Reversing the Trauma of War is exceptional. It is not only a must-read but a must-use both by those suffering with PTSD and by practitioners who work with those who suffer from the ravages of war. I have found it useful both personally and in my practice of treating those who have experienced many forms of trauma. Because of the complex presentation of PTSD, this handbook should be considered a "tool box." It provides personal vignettes and multiple guides to manage the multitude of symptoms associated with PTSD. It has been an honor to review this work for I see it as great resource for all who suffer from and all who treat PTSD.

Brian J. Masterson, MD, MPH, FACP, FACLP
Col, USAF (Ret.), MC, CFS,
FMR Commander, AF Theater Hospital, Balad, Iraq, 2006–2007,
Psychiatry & Internal Medicine

What a gem of a book! *Reversing the Trauma of War* is a gift of hope for veterans and their families whose lives are compromised by trauma and PTSD. While the clear, step-by-step mental imagery exercises are very user-friendly, don't let the simplicity fool you: the practices are grounded in the most recent cutting-edge research to effectively rewire the brain and regulate the nervous system. In my work as a psychotherapist, this book is a valued resource in my practice toolbox, and for my clients.

Leslie Davenport, MA, MS, LMFT
Faculty, California Institute of Integral Studies;
editor, *Transformative Imagery*

Brilliant! The book is amazingly well written, communicates effectively at the appropriate level, is well organized, and includes terrific case studies, great dialogue, and an array of practical exercises that boggle the mind in their variety, cleverness, and detail. I recommend it to everyone — laypersons, undergraduates, mental health professionals, and your next-door neighbor.

Alan S. Kaufman, PhD
Clinical Professor of Psychology,
Yale University, School of Medicine, Child Study Center

What Kahaney and Epstein have achieved is unique. Weaving together an understanding of combat PTSD, personal stories, and an easily accessible guide to self-care and resolution, they offer healing through the simple and powerful tool of mental imagery. A remarkably practical book, the authors break down common themes of combat PTSD, offer simple explanations and provide mental imagery "recipes" that one can easily understand and use immediately.

Randy Kasper, LCSW, PhD
Director, School of Imagery & Health;
Professor of Social Work, California State University

This book presents a novel and powerful way to access painful PTSD memories and images and to transform them. The authors provide you with simple and accessible tools to reverse and correct those images. The visualization exercises allow for the transformation to occur in natural and effortless ways. As a long-term practitioner of this method I can attest to its efficacy and quasi-miraculous healing effects. The authors' voice is gentle and comforting and can be trusted to guide you through the different phases of your recovery.

Catherine Shainberg, PhD
Author, *DreamBirth: Transforming the Journey of Childbirth through Imagery*

Reversing the Trauma of War brings the powerful tool of mental imagery to the forefront in treating PTSD. This exceptionally important book is easy to read and contains a wealth of imagery exercises.

Nicholas E. Brink, PhD
Past President, American Association for the Study of Mental Imagery; author, *Grendel and His Mother*

As part of the healing legacy of Dr. Gerald Epstein, this impressive book is a vital resource for individuals and families coping with post-traumatic stress as well as for clinicians who want to utilize the power of imagination in the therapeutic process.

Ulas Kaplan, EdD
Associate Professor, Lesley University

An extraordinarily useful and practical guide that veterans can easily use to heal from the symptoms of PTSD. Soldiers, sailors and marines can now safely move through latent trauma and come out the other side less reactive, more able to enjoy their life in the present moment.

Anees A. Sheikh, PhD
Past editor, *Journal of Mental Imagery*; Past President, American Association for the Study of Mental Imagery

Reversing the Trauma of War

PTSD Help for Veterans, Active-Duty Personnel and Their Families

Reversing the Trauma of War

PTSD Help for Veterans, Active-Duty Personnel and Their Families

Phyllis Kahaney, MSW, PhD
Rachel Epstein, LAc, JD

ACMI PRESS
New York

Reversing the Trauma of War
PTSD Help for Veterans, Active-Duty Personnel
and Their Families

Copyright © 2020 by Phyllis Kahaney and Rachel Epstein
Book Cover Design & Interior Layout by CenterPointe Media

This book is not intended as a substitute for medical advice from physicians. The reader can consult a physician in matters relating to his or her health and particularly with respect to any symptoms that may require diagnosis or medical attention.

All rights reserved. No part of this work may be reproduced or utilized in any form or by any means, electronic or mechanical, including the internet, photocopying, microfilming, recording, or by an information storage and retrieval system, without permission in writing from the publisher.

Publisher's Cataloging-in-Publication Data
Names: Kahaney, Phyllis, author. | Epstein, Rachel, 1957- author.
Title: Reversing the trauma of war : PTSD help for veterans, active duty personnel and their families / Phyllis Kahaney, Rachel Epstein.
Description: New York : ACMI Press, 2020. | Includes bibliographical references and index.
Identifiers: LCCN 2019944026 (print) |
ISBN 978-1-883148-26-3 (paperback)
ISBN: 978-883148-27-0 (ebook)
Subjects: LCSH: Post-traumatic stress disorder--Treatment. | Psychic trauma--Treatment. | Veterans--Mental health. | Imagery (Psychology) | Stress (Psychology) | Mental health. | BISAC: SELF-HELP / Post-Traumatic Stress Disorder (PTSD) | PSYCHOLOGY / Psychopathology / Post-Traumatic Stress Disorder (PTSD) | PSYCHOLOGY / Mental Health.
Classification: LCC RC552.P67 K35 2019 (print) |
LCC RC552.P67 (ebook) | DDC 616.852/1--dc23.

We are more than our past. We each contain the possibility of overcoming the effects of anything and everything — including war trauma. What follows is a proven method to reverse, in a step-by-step fashion, the difficult challenges of PTSD.

We dedicate this book to the remarkable men and women who have served in the United States military and who have sacrificed themselves for the benefit of us all.

Reversing the Trauma of War

Contents

Acknowledgments xiii
Foreword xv
Preface: Phyllis' Story xix
Preface: Rachel's Story xxiv

Chapter 1:   What Is Mental Imagery 1
Chapter 2:   Healing As Freedom 6
Chapter 3:   How to Practice Mental Imagery 17
Chapter 4:   Hypervigilance 26
Chapter 5:   Anxiety and Fear 35
Chapter 6:   Anger 45
Chapter 7:   Triggers 56
Chapter 8:   Isolation 65
Chapter 9:   Depression 69
Chapter 10: Guilt 79
Chapter 11: Insomnia and Nightmares 91
Chapter 12: Loss and Grief 105
Chapter 13: Physical Pain 112
Chapter 14: Concussions and Mild Traumatic Brain Injury 127

Chapter 15: Overcoming Addiction 135
Chapter 16: Military Sexual Trauma 142
Chapter 17: Life Plan and Stopping Exercises:
             Using Your Will 154
Chapter 18: For the Families of Vets 159
Chapter 19: Creating Your Own Exercises 168
Chapter 20: Choosing to Live Life Well 171
Chapter 21: Notes for Healthcare Professionals: Mental Imagery
             as a Therapeutic Modality 176
Chapter 22: For Clinicians: Techniques to Reverse Nightmares,
             Flashbacks, and Intrusive Memories 180

Endnotes 192
Sources of Imagery 195
References 196
Main Index 201
Index of PTSD Patient Stories 209
Index of Mental Imagery Exercises 210
About the Authors 217

Acknowledgments

We are deeply indebted to the veterans at the San Diego Vet Center who shared their challenges with Phyllis. Their trust in her and their willingness to actively engage in their own healing process shaped Phyllis' understanding of how to tackle, bit by bit, the symptoms of PTSD. Their success in using mental imagery gave Phyllis the impetus to write this book.

This book would not have been possible without the support of Dr. Gerald Epstein, a Vietnam war veteran. His teachings on the therapeutic application of mental imagery form the foundation of this book. The variety and depth of the imagery exercises have been greatly enriched by the inclusion of exercises created by both Dr. Epstein and his teacher, Mme. Colette Aboulker-Muscat. Colette developed her pioneering techniques of reversing trauma while treating victims of war in World War II and other military conflicts.

A warm thank you to all those who read through the book's many drafts and revisions and gave us excellent feedback: Alan Kaufman, Brian Masterson, Arend Westra, Randal Wittry, Brian

Hays, Steven Hartwell, Lola Jordeth, Ellen Roberts, and John Hannides.

A heartfelt thank you to Eva Okada and Stephanie Berger for their invaluable advice for improving the book. Finally, many thanks to Matthew and Joan Greenblatt, our graphic designers, for both their patience and skill, to Joanne Camas, our keen-eyed copyeditor, and to Kristen Berthelotte for her fine indices.

Foreword

We are now at the dawn of a new understanding of how to treat post-traumatic stress disorder (PTSD), an understanding that gives hope to active-duty combatants, veterans, and their families. At the forefront of this new understanding is a particularly potent treatment to alleviate symptoms and restore normalcy called mental imagery.

Combat PTSD has many dimensions that are disruptive to daily life. The effects of PTSD create suffering both for the person dealing with the symptoms and for their family and friends. Too often the suffering overshadows much of the joy of life, leaving people feeling hopeless. This despair brings with it a slew of negative emotions, such as anger and depression, and physical manifestations, like pain and insomnia, all of which work together to perpetuate the cycle of pain and suffering. This book addresses the emotional, physical, and mental symptoms of PTSD through the unique technique of mental imagery. Mental imagery, sometimes called visualization or guided imagery, gently reshapes our memories, reconstructs our sense of self, and transforms our experiences of being in the world. It calms the nervous system, reduces the responsiveness to pain and fear, aids in reestablishing meaningful relationships, and helps a person feel comfortable in their environment once again.

I served as a psychiatrist in the U.S. Army during the 1960s, and I saw firsthand the war trauma created by the Vietnam conflict. At that time, I treated young soldiers returning from 'Nam who were suffering from incredibly severe symptoms of what was then called "war neurosis." During previous wars, this kind of residual combat trauma was called "shell shock" or "neurasthenia" — now it is called PTSD. These combatants came to the wards, overwhelmed by symptoms of PTSD, to be assessed and treated before being discharged from active duty. The standard tranquilizers and antidepressants of the time were entirely inadequate, unable to handle the unending assault of traumatic memories experienced by these young men and women. These memories could be reawakened by various triggers in their civilian surroundings. The treating physicians often felt helpless, knowing that the prescribed medications would not stem the tsunami of despair and desolation that the young people were experiencing.

That was in 1968 to 1970, a number of years before I discovered a new resource in 1974 — mental imagery. Once I understood the remarkable beneficial effects that mental imagery had on patients, mental imagery became the focus and direction of my life's work. Where pills and talk therapy often failed, I found the power of the mind to prevail, serving as a potent medicine. My mentor and teacher, Mme. Colette Aboulker-Muscat, used mental imagery to help victims of World War II and to treat Israeli soldiers suffering from PTSD. She called her technique *retracing the past*. She un-

Foreword

derstood that we cannot change the objective facts of the past, but we *can* change our attitudes to and memories of the past — and thereby our responses to those memories. In this way, we can learn to approach each experience in the present moment, fresh and freed from the traumatic memories and the hypervigilance of war.

This book builds on Phyllis' success in using mental imagery with her patients at the San Diego Vet Center, where she worked as a readjustment counselor. She and Rachel crafted *Reversing the Trauma of War* to provide tools for you to become your own healer by calling on the healthy part of your mind to reverse the effects of post-traumatic stress. Using these quick and powerful short exercises can help you bring balance and order into your life. Additionally, there are imagery exercises specifically to help family members. The appendices teach clinicians several advanced techniques as well.

May this book provide liberation from what was once thought to be an endless, irreversible affliction.

Gerald Epstein, MD
Maj, US Army, MC
Founder, American Institute for Mental Imagery
Assistant Clinical Professor of Psychiatry,
Mt. Sinai Medical Center, NYC

Reversing the Trauma of War

PREFACE
Phyllis' Story

When I was a college student, I spent two years in Jerusalem during a period when there were many bombs and a lot of shooting. In those days, little attention was paid to PTSD. If you survived these war events physically uninjured, you were left to your own devices, while the physically injured were given medical treatment. You were encouraged to get on with your daily life, and for the most part, you did. If anything, I and others like me became greater risk-takers — going into dangerous areas of the Old City, traveling through the West Bank at night, or going with a kibbutz member at midnight to sweep the roads for land mines. I found it all very exciting: Being in danger made me feel alive. And I judged others who were not so daring. I felt that those who were fearful or stuck close to safe places were missing out on the full life of being in the Middle East, with all its possible experiences.

When I got back to the United States after those two years in Jerusalem, however, I noticed a difference in how I reacted to everyday situations. Even though I was living in a small college town in the Midwest, I continued to look for bombs and other explosive devices that might be in abandoned bags, boxes, and trash at the side of the road. I started having nightmares. I was afraid to go to the movies, thinking the people sitting behind me might shoot me in the back of the head. I was edgy at night in the apartment I shared with a friend — every sound made me think someone was breaking into the apartment.

After a year, I graduated and moved to France, where I lived with my boyfriend in a cathedral town that had lots of alleyways and secluded places where people could hide and spring an attack. I became afraid to be alone. I started having what turned out to be anxiety attacks, but I thought I was dying. I had nightmares every night.

When I finally went to the doctor, he told me that I needed to keep busy and suggested that I start cleaning out closets. This doctor made no effort to see if there was an underlying issue causing these symptoms. He simply considered me to be a "neurotic" woman, and his answer to my suffering was to give me Valium. This made me feel drugged, and I found it hard to function. I finally ended up coming back to the States to consult with specialists, who told me that I had an anxiety syndrome. I was taught to do deep breathing and self-hypnosis. These helped me enough to return to France. I was doing better, but I still felt on edge, finding it difficult to be in isolated places.

About ten years later, I was at a small faculty party at the university where I was teaching. There I heard an instructor from the psychology department tell a group of people about the veterans' group he was leading. The description he gave of these veterans sounded like me — they hated to be in crowds, had the

Preface: Phyllis' Story

same nightmare over and over, felt constantly unsafe, searched for explosive devices everywhere, felt uneasy with their backs to the door, and jumped at the slightest sudden sound. I researched PTSD, and over time I understood that it is characterized by three classes of symptoms: an exaggerated startle response, an avoidance of anything that reminds one of the trauma, and unwanted, intrusive thoughts (and sometimes dreams) that remind one of the trauma.

Now that I understood I had these symptoms and reactions, I began searching for help. I started taking yoga classes and learned to meditate. I got a CD to listen to at night when I had a nightmare and couldn't get back to sleep. I arranged my office so the chair faced the door. I continued to avoid big gatherings like the Fourth of July because the loud noise of the fireworks and the crowds made me miserable. I now knew that I would never be the person I had been before being exposed to the violence of war, but I could see that I could get better and be more functional than I felt at that time. In my search for someone who understood PTSD, I met Dr. Gerald Epstein, a New York City psychiatrist who specialized in using mental imagery to treat mental, emotional, and physical ailments. I worked with him off and on for about three years. After doing the imagery exercises or visualizations he prescribed, I began to feel that I was moving toward a place I recognized as myself. I was more relaxed and open with others, much less anxious, able to focus on tasks that were important to me, and less tense and quick-tempered with my family. It felt like the small black-and-white world I had lived in since my time in Israel had transformed into Technicolor. I was awestruck; I hadn't realized how badly I had felt until I got better. I had taken my difficult qualities as "just the way I was," when in fact they were symptoms of a condition. And while I knew I probably wouldn't overcome all the symptoms, I could get much better and live a freer, fuller life.

Out of this experience, I knew I wanted to use mental imagery to help other people. After 25 years as an academic, I went back to school to get a degree in social work, then I got a job at the Vet Center in San Diego. I worked exclusively with combat veterans and their families, all of whom were struggling with the fallout of PTSD. During the four years that I counseled the men and women who had served our country in war, I found out that nearly everyone could improve their PTSD symptoms if they committed to working through their problems: taking medication, doing talk therapy, working in other modalities like Eye Movement Desensitization and Reprocessing (EMDR), tai chi, art therapy, hypnotherapy, somatic experience training, mantra repetition, meditation, yoga — and of course what was becoming my own specialty, mental imagery. It was exciting to see how veterans could move from being barely functional to being very successful in every aspect of their lives, from work, to relationships, to their belief that life could be good. At times, it was like watching a fairy tale unfold where the hero or heroine — Rip Van Winkle, Snow White — would awaken from a long sleep and become once again part of the world instead of divided from it. Often in that "awakening," the veteran rejoined families, took part in community activities, connected to nature, joined a church or synagogue, or in some way began to feel part of something larger than him or herself. For many people, it was the awakening to the experience of spirit.

Preface: Phyllis' Story

Back in 2011, Rachel suggested I write a book about my work at the Vet Center. Together we sketched out a book outline on the back of an envelope. We found that working together was a seamless collaboration: I wrote of my clinical work with combatants using mental imagery as a core treatment modality, and Rachel added background material on mental imagery, created and culled imagery exercises from a trove of sources, and edited the final work. When "I" is used in the text, it is always Phyllis speaking.

PREFACE
Rachel's Story

My father was a psychiatrist, a medical specialty that my old-fashioned, down-to-earth grandmother did not consider to be a "real" doctor. Nonetheless, my father followed his passion and left cardiology to become a "shrink"; he realized that merely treating the physical did not relieve his patients of the distress stemming from their minds. Thus, from an early age I was taught that the mind is a primary source of illness and suffering.

In retrospect, it is not surprising that I spent much of my teen years and twenties looking into meditation, the human potential movement, and bodywork for novel ways to heal body and mind. After college, I worked on Wall Street in the computer sector, but eventually left the field to study Chinese medicine and acupuncture.

Upon meeting my future husband, Jerry Epstein, I knew I had found a true companion with whom I could explore the vastness of mindbody medicine. For the next 30 years, Jerry took me on a magical mystery tour into the world of mental imagery. Here was a pathway to freedom. Working by his side, I learned how people

Preface: Rachel's Story

could harness the power of their minds to heal by simply picturing something. While appearing magical, this process is in fact grounded in modern science.

In contrast to Phyllis, I embraced trauma work not through any personal suffering but from my work as a healthcare professional. As an acupuncturist, my practice included highly sensitive individuals who often displayed wide swings in their ability to self-regulate physically and emotionally. With both needles and images I cared for my patients.

I found that trauma was experienced on a continuum from minor early childhood scars to major inhibitions brought on by emotional abuse, physical assault, financial ruin, natural catastrophe and, of course, the trauma of war.

Over the years, I came to recognize more fully that though we believe and act as if there is a separation between mind and body, there is none. They are merely two sides of the same coin. Trauma is locked in the body as much as in the mind — and both must be freed. Mental imagery bridges this abyss to stimulate our natural inborn capacity to heal.

When I first learned of Phyllis' work at the San Diego Vet Center, I immediately felt drawn to work with her to create a book specifically for the American armed forces to teach them this powerful self-healing technique. I was intrigued by the way she chose to gradually peel away trauma by introducing small changes that had a reorganizing ripple effect in the individual's experience of daily life. Through many years of working with imagery, it had become clear to me that *simple is powerful*, and *less is more*.

In writing this book, I have come to see that the miracle of leading a 'normal' life is truly within reach of even the most traumatized and wounded amongst us. All it takes to begin is a sliver of hope.

CHAPTER 1

What Is Mental Imagery?

The best definition of mental imagery is the mind thinking in pictures. In our daily lives, we see all around us examples of people using mental imagery with a particular goal in mind. Athletes who visualize the baseball flying out of the park before the ball is even thrown; the cancer patient imagining healthy cells overtaking unhealthy cells; the job candidate imagining how the interview will go well before stepping into the interview room. All of these, when used consistently, have been shown in controlled studies to improve outcomes.

Imaginal thinking is different from the logical thinking we are taught in school and later in our work. Logical thinking helps us communicate through words or do other practical things, like operating machines. But thinking logically is not the only way we use our minds. Consider all the times you have solved a problem or discovered something *non*-logically — maybe in a dream, or in a flash of insight while driving or walking. At those times we are thinking, but not necessarily in a logical, sequential way. This other kind of imaginal thinking allows scientists to come up with new ideas, or doctors to find keys to an illness, or artists to discover the story they are trying to tell in pictures. Whereas logical thinking is used to manage contact with the world outside ourselves, mental imagery helps us make contact with our inner reality. Intuition and mental imagery are mediated through the right cerebral hemisphere, whereas logical-sequential thought is mediated through the left hemisphere.

This book teaches you how to use mental imagery to overcome the symptoms of PTSD — symptoms such as anxiety, depression, hypervigilance, nightmares, and anger. Also included are imagery exercises for sexual trauma (a hidden epidemic in the military), as well as a chapter to help family members cope with the stress of living with someone suffering from PTSD. This book can be safely and easily used at home. These exercises lay a basis for you to start to do your own healing. I am not suggesting that doing these exercises replaces seeing your doctor, taking prescribed medication, or engaging in other mental health treatments. Instead, doing mental imagery offers a method to work independently on your own while engaging with other practices. In the same way, imagery work dovetails nicely with any religious practice or belief. In fact, imagery has been a central part of most religions around the world including Christianity, Judaism, Islam, Tibetan Buddhism, Shamanism and many others. Imagery can be seen as a type of nonverbal prayer.

Each chapter of the book is organized so that you:
- Understand the issue being addressed;
- See how other combat veterans have dealt with a similar situation;

What Is Mental Imagery?

- Choose a specific imagery exercise to overcome a particular symptom or group of symptoms.

By practicing mental imagery for less than a minute two or three times a day, you can cope more effectively with stressful situations and slowly shift away from the automatic reactions that seem etched in your body and mind. With continued practice, you create a new way of being in the world. Life itself becomes different as you live your life and understand your experiences differently. By using mental imagery to transform your understanding and behavior, you can become free.

In fact, mental imagery, like meditation and other mental practices, rewires your brain. Scientists call this ability to reorganize and form new neural connections in the brain and nervous system *neuroplasticity*. The *neuro* refers to the nerve cells that make up the brain and nervous system; *plasticity* refers to the brain and nervous system's capacity to be pliable and malleable through exposure to new experiences. Just as you learned and adapted to war through neuroplasticity, you can unlearn this behavior as well.

War trauma is an extreme manifestation of what Dr. Robert Rhondell Gibson[1] termed the *false emergency state*. The emergency state is a fight-or-flight response to a life-threatening situation, such as facing a lion in the jungle or being robbed at gunpoint. In meeting an emergency, our body is flooded with hormones gearing us up to either fight or run. Our heart races, sweat pours out, our muscles contract, we're ready for action. The sympathetic nervous system — the part of our nervous system geared to act — takes over. After the fight or the flight experience, we relax and rest, falling into the parasympathetic nervous system's repose and regaining our balance.

Of course, the hypervigilance that manifests from combat stress is an adaptive habitual response to being in a true constant state of emergency. This response to imminent danger becomes ingrained in both body and mind — in the nervous system, muscles, thoughts, feelings, and perceptions. It becomes the combatant's go-to response, and after a while, it doesn't take much stimulus to elicit this reaction in either a war zone or back at home.

In modern civilian life, however, at least in the Western world, we rarely encounter times when our life is truly in jeopardy. Too often we experience every distressing daily event as an "emergency" — a huge generalized stress response. From the alarm clock going off in the morning, mistaking it for a bomb, to feeling trapped in stop-and-go traffic, or mistaking trees along the side of the road as hiding places for enemies, the slightest stimulus can take us into an emergency state — back into a time and place that doesn't exist now. Almost all of the day-to-day emergencies that we perceive are in fact *false emergencies*, where the events are not life-threatening. So the torrential release of stress hormones, when there is no true emergency, has no function in our everyday life; instead, these hormones turn into poisons that our bodies need to eliminate. Over years, this overtaxing of our bodily systems leads to physical pain, disease, and debility.

The good news is that with regular practice, mental imagery tones down our nervous system so we become less hypervigilant, less fearful, and less anxious. We learn to feel safer and more at ease in the world. We learn to read our perceptions of the envi-

What Is Mental Imagery?

ronment in a new way, without the preconceptions of our war experience that color the truth of the present moment. Now when we are anxious or angry, we can ask ourselves, "Is this really an emergency? Is my life being threatened right now?"

In sum, the benefits of mental imagery are numerous. It is quick, easy, and pleasant. It happens so fast that it appears to be in no time. It costs nothing and is available to everyone. This collection offers exercises that are very gentle, stimulate healing, and are designed not to trigger strong negative emotions. However, if at any point you feel you need to seek help from a trained professional, do so. If you have questions about the imaginal process, you can contact the authors or other trained imaginal therapists.

While most of this manual focuses on imaginal exercises, we have included two other techniques: *Life Plan* and *Stopping Exercises* that you can use alone or in addition to practicing imagery. These techniques focus on using your will to actively change reactive emotional responses, habits, and addictive cravings. There are also a few exercises that involve physical activity, like smelling a pleasing scent or carrying a stone or amulet with you. Many people have found these helpful. Finally, this book would not be complete without a chapter teaching you the tools to create your own imagery.

We hope you'll discover, as we have, that there are few difficulties that can't be ameliorated through the power of imagination and will.

CHAPTER 2

Healing As Freedom

On a cold Thursday in November, when the waiting room at the Vet Center was almost empty, a staff member asked me to do an intake for a combat veteran from the Korean conflict who had appeared just moments before and looked so uneasy they were afraid he might not stay.

There in the corner was an exceptionally well-dressed gentleman of around 75. Most of our veterans came to the center dressed casually in jeans and a T-shirt and went by their first name, but this veteran had on a dress shirt, tie, and sport coat. When I called his name, he rose, straightened his lapels, and reached out to shake my hand, introducing himself as Mr. James.

Back in my office, Mr. James explained that yesterday "something terrible" had happened. While walking with his friend from the car to a restaurant, an airplane that was landing at a regional airport flew just over his head. Without thinking, he hit the ground, believing he was under attack. After picking himself up and glancing over at his puzzled friend, he was so embarrassed that he made an excuse to leave and didn't go through with the lunch.

Hitting the ground at the sudden sound of an airplane overhead

Healing As Freedom

wasn't all that was wrong, he said. He told me that he was unable to sleep for more than two hours at a time, was always looking over his shoulder at the slightest of sounds, was easily angered, and had started having nightmares. All these symptoms were particularly bad at this time of year, he said, and because of this, he had grown to hate the holidays. His dislike of Thanksgiving and Christmas had always been a trial for his wife and three children, but in recent years it had become worse.

"What's the matter with me?" he asked. "I feel like I'm losing my mind."

This is a common story with combat veterans — they experience physical and emotional symptoms that often get worse at a particular time of year, such as around the anniversary of a battle or the death of a comrade, or the date when they were wounded. Such behavior often comes as a surprise to veterans and their families, and it makes it hard to lead an ordinary life.

Over a period of weeks, we began to explore what was happening in this veteran's life. It became clear that Mr. James' symptoms were at their worst during the winter holiday season. He experienced a great deal of shame about these symptoms and chose to hide everything from his beloved wife, whom he wanted to protect. Though he had been a fairly successful businessman, these symptoms had prevented him from achieving his full potential; and at this point the psychological toll of it all was becoming overwhelming.

What happens to a person when they are in combat is complex and unpredictable. There are so many factors to consider. Where on the ship was the person located when it was bombed? Was the veteran in charge of other sailors, Marines, or soldiers? Was the person physically wounded? Had there been other traumas in the person's life before the incident — the sudden death of a parent, for example, or a serious automobile accident? Was the traumatic event a one-time occurrence, or was that person exposed to many such incidents? Answering these questions helps to situate the way someone experiences what happened, how they think about it in the present, and how they can begin to recover.

In Mr. James' case, he had been coping for many years, but this year the symptoms were much worse. Young warriors were still serving in the war in the Middle East and because of that and his recent radiation treatments for cancer, Mr. James had begun to feel the same stress and distress as he had felt right after the war he had fought in so many years ago. His psyche was back on board ship, and he was, every day and every night, 60-plus years later, fighting for his emotional life.

Coming to an Understanding

The relationship between our inner beliefs and our experience of outer events was something I myself knew well, something that Mr. James was beginning to discover for himself. As he consistently practiced the mental imagery exercises every day, he began to experience his beliefs reshaping themselves. And something else became clear to him as well: a growing understanding of the holographic or global nature of the way the mind heals itself. He saw that if he worked with mental imagery on one thing — for example, patterns of anxiety — then other problems began to resolve as well, and he was getting less angry and spending less time isolating himself from others. It's as if in opening a small window, the whole house begins to be filled with light and soon the other windows and doors open on their own.

Perhaps most surprising to Mr. James was that all of this appeared to take place outside of time — that is, correcting the problem through mental imagery was enough to create its reversal so that months and years of doing this kind of therapy were not necessarily required. Some people need more time to process than others, but the process can go quickly, so that sometimes a person needs to come for only a few sessions in order for change to take place. For Mr. James, only four months were necessary. And when he was feeling better and didn't need to come anymore for treatment, he stated that he wrote down these four things on a pad on his desk so he'd remember them:

1. In imagination, anything can happen. This work is about sensitivity, not rules and logic.
2. The past doesn't dictate the future.
3. Healing takes place in action. Use your mind in an active way.
4. The mental and the physical act together as a whole.

What he came to see most profoundly is that this process of healing from combat stress is about freedom — freedom to be as we are and at the same time to be open to change. Magically, when doing this imagery work, we begin to see new possibilities for ourselves. I liken the reality of our life to an inner garden: When we engage in a regular practice of imagery, we are tending to our inner garden of thoughts, beliefs, and perceptions, planting new seeds of hope and action, and removing the unwanted weeds of our habitual post-traumatic-stress responses to everyday life situations. Mental imagery always starts from where we are; we don't deny the "is-ness" of the pain or suffering. However, once it's acknowledged and accepted, we can plant new possibilities for ourselves through the use of mental imagery. Like any gardener, we regularly water our plants, pull up the weeds, and then leave the plants to grow. We keep ourselves focused in the moment, on the action of gardening, not on the end result of the harvest. Likewise, when we practice imagery, we have an intention, aim, or desire to heal from PTSD. But we keep our attention focused in the moment doing the imagery, not on the outcome. As soon as we start focusing on the outcome, we are in the future and will start to feel anxious.

You may find, as Mr. James did, that as you practice mental imagery, you begin to develop the capacity to respond to daily life stressors in a more balanced manner. It's as if you develop the capacity to look at everything as "fact," as it is, without adding judgments or stories about how you or another *should* act or how things *should* be. I worked with a vet who was very angry; he would drink, become angrier, and blame his girlfriend, his father, his college professors, and the war for his anger. As we worked together, we looked at the anger itself rather than the *reason why* he was angry. Once he accepted the anger as a "fact," without attaching the anger to "a story" or a reason for his anger, he was able to overcome the anger. Instead of acting out, drinking, and yelling, he was able to use words and truly communicate with others. He came to understand that the less he blamed others or events, the more empowered he was to reason, to intuit, and to act for his own benefit.

We have been educated to attain and to attach to things. We attain knowledge, wealth, status, stability, material possessions, etc. We attach to our identities (who we think we are), our emotional responses, our points of view, our jobs, our homes, our bank accounts, etc. We mistake ourselves for our opinions, our feelings, and the material objects we own. *Most particularly, we attach to our past, to our life story.* When we attach to our past, we are filled with regret about what should have been. Dwelling in the past leads us to feel depressed. In the same way, attaching or thinking about the future — how it should or ought to be — leaves us feeling anxious. Often we create a story in our heads that the future will continue along the same path as the past, with no change. This storyline leads to inaction, and we feel stuck. In the practice of mental imagery, however, we stay in the moment, freed from regrets of the past and fears of what might be in the future.

When we begin to see life's events, even the most difficult ones, as "fact," without adding judgments (such as "everything is bad and will only get worse"), we facilitate our healing. We don't deny the historical fact, but we don't heap more storyline on top of it. When we shift out of emergency mode, we see what is (the "fact"), gain clarity, and can "let go" of the blame, the past regrets, and the idea that nothing can change. I call this "direct seeing." In fact, when I start working with clients, I explain to them that *the past does not exist.* I am not referring to the concrete events of our personal life history. Nor am I referring to navigating the practical world where we ground ourselves in calendar time of past, present, and future. Rather, I am referring to our inner subjective life where we access memories of the past. In truth, *the past does not exist in this moment of now, only our created memories recall the past.* Our memories are malleable, open to new interpretations and understanding, and can be remembered in a new way. Mental imagery excels at reshaping our ideas of how things were and how things will be.

The beauty of mental imagery is its adaptability to just about any difficulty we face. Here are several examples of how veterans creatively applied it constructively in their lives.

❖

Austin was a veteran of the war in Iraq who had been unable to attend church since he returned to San Diego after completing his third tour of duty. Going to church with his family was important to him, but he found that being around so many people in the large church was too much for him. I gave him this imagery exercise to practice: Austin imagines himself arriving early to church to avoid being jostled by the crowd. He finds a seat at the end of a pew in the back of the church and takes note of the exits so he can leave easily if he wants or needs to. Then he imagines himself in church breathing deeply and fully and feeling calm and centered as the church service progresses. He sees himself filling with light as the choir sings, and then he sees himself calm and reflective while the sermon is being delivered. He sees himself feeling happy and confident as he imagines walking up the aisle to receive communion. He imagines doing this with the knowledge that at any time he can

Healing As Freedom

leave church if his anxiety becomes overwhelming.

Austin did this imagery exercise three times a day for the week before he attended church the following Sunday. He drove to the church and sat in his car and did some breathing exercises as the church began to fill. He had asked his brother to go on ahead to reserve the seat Austin wanted at the end of the back pew. Austin came into the church just after the service had begun. He slipped into the spot next to his brother and enjoyed the service until almost the end. At that point, he signaled his brother that he was leaving, because he didn't want to walk out in a crowd.

Over the next several weeks, Austin continued to do the imagery exercise three times a day until, after six weeks, he was able to be in church without feeling panicked. Eventually, he was able to use these skills in other social settings — parties, concerts, college classrooms — no longer feeling the need to avoid the things he had previously enjoyed before the war.

❖

Amanda was a 34-year-old former gunnery sergeant who was going to school full-time, working part-time, and taking care of her 3-year-old daughter. She came into my office looking exhausted and said that she was unable to sleep.

She drank eight cups of coffee each day "to keep going," but all that caffeine made it impossible for her to sleep at night when she badly needed to rest. On top of that, she didn't schedule one minute of her day to relax — she was always doing household chores, working, or studying.

Together we came up with a plan for her to slowly reduce her intake of coffee until she had one caffeinated cup in the morning and then only decaf after that. She began to sleep. Then we worked on short breathing exercises in moments of stress as well as imagery exercises that she used on a daily basis to make long-term changes. Within a month she reported "feeling better than I have in a long time." After six weeks of working together, she said she no longer needed to come in for treatment. She was feeling "wonderful" and her life was "back on track." She said she was particularly struck by the fact that she knew how to use all these skills and that they had become a natural part of her life. She didn't need to "schedule them" and get anxious about them, because after a couple of weeks of practice, they had become second nature. With these tools, she was able to finish her last year of college and graduate, feel productive at work, and, most important of all, spend quality time with her partner and her child.

❖

Joe, a veteran who had recently returned from serving in Afghanistan, was having trouble at work. He managed a busy store, with many people coming and going throughout the day. Being around so many people overwhelmed him. We began our work focusing on simple breathing exercises to help calm him. After two office visits, he reported he was able to take a minute or two several times throughout the day and go into a supply closet, do a breathing exercise, and then come out to the sales floor again, feeling refreshed and anxiety-free. He was able to use such moments of focused breathing at home and in social situations until, after several weeks, he felt he had control of his symptoms and was gaining control over his life in general.

Sometimes it can be enough to do breathing exercises or change simple behavior patterns, but to make permanent shifts in ourselves, I prescribe imagery exercises that include a few rounds of relaxed breathing before imaging. The whole process takes just seconds to a minute to do. Sitting with closed eyes in an upright posture and taking several rounds of relaxing breaths helps to turn our senses inward so we can make new discoveries. It is best to be in a quiet place without distracting noise or music so that our attention can stay inward. In a sense, we are giving ourselves positive triggers for change. Generally, we practice imagery three times a day for 21 days. This rhythmic repetition imprints a new way of being in ourselves, similar to the way we can fix a coding bug in a computer program.

To sum up, the benefits of imagery are many. Imagery makes us active participants in our own healing, in which we can change our attitude toward our life. This change in attitude, in turn, allows us to see more clearly and gain more control. In working with a particular issue through imagery, a holographic effect is created: By working with a part, we are healing the whole. We are empowered to become stronger, healthier, more directed, self-confident, and able to form healthy relationships. All this happens when practicing mental imagery — something that is available at any time and is quick and cost-effective, with no adverse side effects.

In working with mental imagery, our aim is to create inner freedom. So many of the symptoms of PTSD make us feel unfree

— isolation, inability to control anger impulses, suffering when in crowds, fighting nightmares while asleep...the list goes on and on. In order to create inner freedom, we practice imagery exercises that at first allow us to become more directed, more self-confident, and increasingly feel more in charge of our health.

Ultimately, this book is a manual that invites you to reconsider the way you live in the world, to create new ground rules for living your life, for being here *now*. And most of all, it provides you — active combatants, veterans, and anyone who has suffered from war trauma — with a road map to let go of the past.

There are six cardinal rules in this healing method:
1. Having PTSD is not a sign of weakness.
2. There are NO judgments or worries about how you or others ought to behave, act, or be in the world.
3. Live in the present moment — the past and future do NOT exist. The past is gone, and the future has yet to be.
4. There is always hope and the possibility of change.
5. There is always a safe haven to be found.
6. Be your own authority and listen to your own inner wisdom.

In the next chapters, through your own experimentation, you will learn new ways to live your life in a way that allows you to become resilient — stronger, healthier, more directed, self-confident, and whole.

CHAPTER 3

How to Practice Mental Imagery

This chapter teaches you the basics for doing imagery: how to sit, how to breathe, what time of day to practice, and how often. There are also two short "practice" imagery exercises to show you just how easy it is to do. Finally, we've shared some pointers to help if you find it difficult to visualize. After reading this chapter, you are free to jump to any chapter that interests you.

Step 1. How to sit: Find a quiet place to practice. Sit up straight in a comfortable chair (ideally one with armrests), with both feet on the floor. Keeping your shoulders relaxed, put each arm on your lap or on an armrest, with your back straight against the back of the chair. The way you sit is important as a straight spine keeps you comfortably focused. Now, close your eyes. Feel the quiet if you can. Then turn your attention to your breathing.

Step 2. How to breathe: You may have noticed that when you are under stress, you tend to hold your breath. To reverse this habit and get into a light, relaxed state, you take three rounds of relaxed breathing *prior* to doing the imagery exercises. Here are two different ways of breathing we recommend to start off the imagery. Both start with your focus on the outbreath or exhalation.

a) **Classic breathing technique:** Sitting up, close your eyes, and start by breathing out a long, slow exhalation through your mouth then breathe in normally through your nose; again, breathe out a long, slow exhalation through your mouth then a normal inhalation through your nose; follow this with a third round of breathing, a long, slow exhalation through your mouth and a normal inhalation through the mouth. So you are doing this special *long outbreaths, normal inbreaths* for a total of three rounds of breathing. (See Dr. Epstein demonstrate this breathing technique at https://www.youtube.com/watch?v=UBNUqLdLkSw.)

OR

b) **Three magic outbreaths:** Sitting up, close your eyes, purse your lips, and gently *blow out* three short breaths. Do not breathe in — just slowly and softly breathe out three times. For many people, this is enough to establish an immediate relaxation response. It's one of my favorites, as I find it the simplest and quickest way to relax and focus.

Why exhale first? It calms your nervous system and reverses your normal shallow inhalation/exhalation pattern. These breathing exercises rid your body of two waste products: carbon dioxide

How to Practice Mental Imagery

and the stress hormone norepinephrine. Your breathing, heartbeat, and thoughts slow down, and when you are calm, you become open to new ways of thinking, feeling, and acting. In this more relaxed state, you are able to turn your senses inward, to what is happening inside yourself, in the form of pictures. The relaxed breathing should take a few seconds.

> *Bottom line:* Don't get caught up in whether you are breathing "correctly." If you find you need to breathe in before you breathe out, that's okay, too. The breathing is simply a stepping stone to the imagery.

Step 3. Follow the imagery exercise: There are many choices of imagery exercises for a particular difficulty. Read through them and pick the one that you'd like to work on. Start with shorter imagery exercises. After you build your "imagery muscle," try some of the longer exercises. Pretty soon you will be making up your own imagery exercises!

Step 4. Breathe out and open your eyes: At the end of the imagery exercise, breathe out (exhale) once and open your eyes.

More pointers for practicing imagery:
    Make an audio recording of the imagery: You may prefer to record the imagery exercise you are working with on your smartphone so you can play it back the first several times you practice

the exercise. Or you can ask someone to read it to you as you do it. After a few times of hearing it, you will probably recall it from memory.

When to practice imagery: Imagery is best done in a rhythmic fashion at the same time each day:
- In the morning, upon awakening (or before breakfast);
- In the evening, at twilight, as the sun is setting (or before dinner);
- Before going to bed.

These three times are natural prayer and meditation times, potent transition points when we are most open to listening to our inner wisdom. While most imagery exercises are done three times a day, some are done only once or twice a day, and a few are done only in the moment you feel distressed.

If you have trouble remembering to do the imagery, set an alarm on your phone. And if you forget to do an imagery exercise, just do it when you remember. If you find you can't do it three times a day, do it twice a day, in the morning and before bed.

How long does each imagery exercise take? Less is more. Most imagery exercises are short and take only seconds to a minute. There are a couple of longer exercises that may take a few minutes to complete. *Bottom line:* Do *not* concern yourself with setting a timer, just let the process flow naturally.

How many days do I practice an imagery exercise? Most

imagery exercises are done three times a day for 21 days. Occasionally some are done for just seven days once or twice a day. Feel free to continue doing an exercise past 21 days, but always take a seven-day break after each 21-day cycle so you don't become habituated to it.

How many issues do I work on at the same time? Work on only one issue at a time: You can choose to do one or more imagery exercises as long as they deal with the same issue. Always open your eyes after an imagery exercise before you start the next one.

Setting an intention: Each imagery exercise starts by stating an aim or inner instruction for what you want to achieve, such as to curb anger, drive calmly, feel safe, or let go of guilt. Silently state the name of the exercise and the intention each time before beginning the exercise.

What if I meditate regularly? Try stopping the daily meditation while you are doing imagery; or at minimum, do the imagery exercise before you meditate.

> *Remember to be patient:* Be consistent in your practice. You are creating new neurological pathways and establishing new mind/body habits. Like building muscles, reps are important and are built over time.

Putting it all together: Here are two short imagery exercises for you to practice that demonstrate both the classic breathing technique and the "three magic breaths" technique.

IMAGERY EXERCISES

The Seashore

Intention: To relax.
Frequency: One time only.

Close your eyes and breathe out three times slowly (e.g., breathe out a long, slow exhalation through the mouth, followed by a normal inhalation through the nose; breathe out a second long, slow breath through the mouth, followed by a normal inhalation through the nose; breathe out a third long, slow exhalation through the mouth). Imagine you are at the beach. See the blue of the sea merge with the blue of the sky at the horizon. Feel the golden warm sand beneath your feet. Hear the sound of the waves and the cries of the seagulls. Touch the water, smell the salty air. Breathe out and open your eyes.

Cleansing Shower

Intention: To cleanse yourself.
Frequency: One time only.

Close your eyes and breathe out three times slowly (e.g., purse your lips, and gently blow out three short breaths. Do not breathe in — just slowly and softly breathe out three times). See and sense yourself stepping into a shower. Turning the water on to a comfortable temperature, feel the water cascading from the showerhead onto your head, shoulders, and back. Sense and feel the water run down your entire body, washing away any impurities into the drain below. When you are clean, step out of the shower and wrap yourself in a white robe. Breathe out and open your eyes.

❖

Tips for Imaging: Engaging All Your Senses

You may have noticed that the imagery asked you to engage *all* your senses inwardly — to see, sense, smell, taste, touch, hear, and feel. Some people see themselves in the imagery (like watching a movie of yourself), others experience themselves in the imagery (like being the actor in a movie instead of viewing themselves in the movie), and still others do both (they see themselves and experience themselves in the imagery). It's all good. There is no right or wrong.

Some people are stronger imagers than others, *but we all have an inborn capacity to imagine,* and the more you do it, the more you develop your imaging muscle. Images appear quickly and disappear just as quickly. You only need a nanosecond of an image to evoke change.

If you had difficulty with the **Seashore** or **Cleansing Shower** exercises, here are some tips that might help you.[2]

1) Look at pictures or photographs of natural settings for 20 to 30 seconds, then close your eyes and see the same pictures appear in your mind.

2) With your eyes open, remember a pleasant scene from your past, then close your eyes and remember these same images.

3) Use your nonvisual senses. For example, close your eyes and hear fish frying in a skillet or the applause of an audience or glasses clinking; or close your eyes and physically smell perfumes or essences of varying strengths. What do these smells evoke?

4) Rely on the senses you use or respond to most easily. For example, if you're an auditory person, hear the sound of the ocean and sense what visual images emerge. When you consciously focus your attention on one sense, you spontaneously evoke other sensory experiences.

5) Some people have the habit of verbalizing rather than visualizing, turning images quickly into words. If this applies to you, practice looking around at your environment for a few minutes without naming, labeling, or categorizing what you see. If you reflexively start to name things, just return to the practice of seeing without further elabora-

tion. Over time, you will find the images emerge more and more spontaneously.

To Recap

- Work on one difficulty at a time. Pick one, two, or three imagery exercises that resonate with you.

- Find a quiet place to practice imagery.

- Sit up in a straight-backed chair with feet on the floor and arms relaxed on each armrest or on your lap.

- Close your eyes and breathe out three times slowly (either the classic breathing or the three magic breaths).

- Do the imagery — Let yourself receive the images effortlessly.

- When you are finished with an exercise, breathe out once and open your eyes.

CHAPTER 4

Hypervigilance

Dustin, a 23-year-old corporal from Tulsa, comes into my office warily. I watch as he stands in front of each window in the office — there are six of them — and looks out each one as though he is scouting for enemy combatants. When I tell him he can sit anywhere he wants, he chooses the chair that is right next to the door. Throughout the intake session, he never stops scanning the office — his eyes are always in motion, and he sits on the very edge of his seat.

"How long have you been back in California?" I ask him.

"Just over four weeks, ma'am," he says, his eyes still scouting the room.

"What was your job in Iraq?"

"Team leader, ma'am. Me and my team of three men went from house to house in each village looking for insurgents."

Dustin has come to the Vet Center, he says, because his wife told him he needed to get help or the marriage was over. He said he wasn't sleeping even two hours a night; he was up all night guarding the front door of their apartment. He didn't trust anyone; he thought his wife was foolish for not being more suspicious of

Hypervigilance

everyone she met. He would drift off to sleep for an hour or two around dawn, and then he would usually wake up with a start, feeling he was under attack from the enemy; and when he reflexively went to reach for his weapon and it wasn't there, he would panic.

He said he couldn't bear to be out among people. He had tried for a couple of weeks to attend college classes, but he was unable to be in the classroom with so many strangers. Now he was taking all his courses by distance learning, even though he found he couldn't focus. He only left home when he had to. Worst of all was driving, because it brought out all his wartime anxieties; drivers speeding past him might try to shoot him, bits of debris lying on the side of the road might be hiding IEDs (improvised explosive devices), people driving or walking across overpasses might try to fire on him, the trees lining the side of the street might be hiding snipers. So he drove very fast, never letting anyone get too close behind him. This constant vigilance, along with the continued lack of sleep and constant watchfulness, left him perpetually exhausted.

This young soldier, fresh from combat, showed the classic symptoms of war trauma that can later turn into PTSD. At the moment, he was struggling with hypervigilance, the constant and exhausting scanning of one's environment for potential threats. He also described feeling guilty that he wasn't still with his buddies in combat. He was unable to sleep, and when he did, he had horrible nightmares about the war. He confided that he was unable to relax, had a hair-trigger temper, and required absolute order at home.

"Well," I said to Dustin, "what do you need?"

"Ma'am," he replied, "all I really want is to be the way I was before the war."

Dustin's hypervigilance is one of the most common responses to having been in combat. In order to survive the many kinds of situations combatants find themselves in, they learn to be aware of their surroundings and ready to take action at any moment. This means it is imperative for combatants to have their weapons at all times and never be off guard. While this kind of action is necessary to survive combat, it is not helpful for daily life as a civilian. For Dustin and his team, who searched buildings in an enemy zone, this intense alertness had been necessary for their safety. But as a civilian in California, it was no longer helpful or useful for Dustin to believe the enemy was everywhere and to behave as if they were.

Similarly, it is unlikely there will be snipers at the supermarket, or roadside bombs on the way to work, or assassins trying to storm the front door of our homes. But after months or even years of living with extra vigilance, it is difficult to lose the habit of watchfulness.

How can we change this entrenched behavior that has become an ingrained habit? By replacing a negative habit with a positive one. We lay down this new habit through a mental imagery exercise. I call this making a correction. In fact, most imagery is a form of correction where we replace an old habit, memory, or belief with a new one. In correcting past painful memories, we are not correcting the fact; we are correcting the *memory* of the fact. Memories are very malleable and can be written over, just like a computer writes over old unneeded code. So in rewriting our memories of the past, we do not dishonor ourselves or others. Instead, we give ourselves permission to live and adapt to this moment freely, without being caught in a loop of dysfunctional memory. Once the memory is corrected, our physical and emotional responses are quieted and no longer activated as quickly. Eventually, with practice, the habitual response is deactivated. Remember, even with the most ingrained instinctual habits, we always have the choice to make this correction.

Dustin said he wanted to change the way he responded to his environment, so we began a series of imaginal exercises. I explained that it takes 21 days to change a habit and that much of his learned behavior was habitual. Because driving was the most troubling problem he was having, he decided to begin with exercises around hypervigilance and driving his car. He did one or two exercises each day for 21 days. He then took a break for seven days. Then he chose a new set of exercises for particular issues that came up and did those for another 21 days, and so on. We worked for several months together, and by the end he had become more relaxed, was sleeping better, and was far less angry when interacting with people.

As with all imagery exercises, we began by my asking Dustin to sit in the upright position — both feet flat on the floor, arms on the chair armrests or hands resting on knees, sitting up straight and tall — and inwardly to state his intention to feel safe while driving. He then took three rounds of abdominal breaths and began the imagery.

IMAGERY EXERCISES FOR HYPERVIGILANCE

This first exercise takes its name from the biblical story of the exodus of the Israelites from Egypt. God separates the Red Sea into two walls of water, leaving a clear passage for the Israelites to cross through the sea safely.

The Red Sea Parting/Safe Passage

Intention: To not feel hemmed in; to feel safe while driving.
Frequency: Morning, evening, and before bed for 21 days.

Close your eyes and breathe out three times slowly. See and sense yourself driving on the road, feeling hemmed in by the other cars around you. Breathe out one time. Now, see this "Red Sea" of cars opening up around you, leaving a clear, safe path for you to drive through unharmed. Breathe out and open your eyes.

> *Note:* If you become anxious while driving, take three quieting breaths (either the three magic breaths or three classic breaths). Then, WITH EYES OPEN and staying alert to the traffic, *for just a moment,* see in your mind's eye the image of the parting of the sea to remind yourself to remain calm and centered.

Hypervigilance

The Tidal Wave

Intention: To navigate safely and calmly among crowds.
Frequency: Morning, evening, and before bed for 21 days, and at other times as needed.

Close your eyes and breathe out three times slowly. See the throngs of people as a tidal wave moving toward you. Now see yourself leap, fly, or being lifted up to the crest of the wave, riding it like a pro surfer, using the wave's energy to surf freely on the waters. Sense and feel that you do *not* need to control the wave, just to flow with it and above it. Breathe out one time.

See the tidal wave gradually losing momentum and strength, ebbing away, as you ride it safely onto the beach, knowing that you and your loved ones are safe and sound. Breathe out and open your eyes.

> *Note:* As you practice the exercises, you'll notice that the imagery may shift and shorten. For example, after a time, you may find yourself surfing the waves when you feel stressed without seeing the tidal wave first.

Steel Wall

Intention: To feel protected when you sense danger.
Frequency: Morning, evening, and before bed for 21 days.

Close your eyes and breathe out three times slowly. Imagine a huge 100-foot-high steel wall between you and what you perceive as dangerous. Know that this wall protects you, keeping you safe at all times. Breathe out and open your eyes.

Ring of Fire

Intention: To feel protected in a threatening situation.
Frequency: Use as often as needed.

With your eyes opened or closed, breathe out slowly three times. Put an imaginal ring of fire around you whenever you feel you are in a threatening situation. Breathe out (and open your eyes if they are closed), keeping this ring of fire around you until you are out of danger.

When the danger has passed (with eyes opened or closed), breathe out three times and imaginally remove the ring of fire.

> *Note:* Remember to imaginally remove the ring of fire when you feel you are out of danger.

The Superhero

Intention: To overcome anxiety when faced with a difficult situation.
Frequency: Use as often as needed.

Close your eyes and breathe out three times. Put on a white silk cape and fly above whatever is causing difficulty. As you look down, say "Shazam" and know that you can rise above anything. Breathe out and open your eyes.

De-armoring

Intention: To become less hypervigilant, less guarded.
Frequency: Every morning for 21 days. This exercise may take a minute or more the first week then less time as you keep doing it. (You can, of course, do it twice or three times a day if you prefer.)

Close your eyes and breathe out three times slowly. See yourself standing before a gate wearing a suit of armor — the one you wear to protect yourself from the world. Breathe out one time and begin removing the armor piece by piece, beginning with the helmet, putting all the pieces behind you and seeing yourself naked.

Breathe out one time. Open the gate and enter into the garden, closing the gate behind you. Find yourself in a luxuriant garden full of birds, flowers, and trees. Listen to the birds singing and smell the fragrance of the flowers.

See a clear pool in the center of the garden. Enter the clean, crystal-clear water and cleanse yourself thoroughly. Come out of the pool, then dive in once again, going to the bottom, where you find something of importance to you. Bring this up to the surface with you and leave the pool. Find a brand-new set of clothes to put on near the pool. What color are the clothes? Afterward, leave the garden through the gate, closing it behind you. Breathe out and open your eyes.

Self-Renewal

Intention: To be the way you were before combat; to be the self you want to be.
Frequency: Every morning for 21 days.

Close your eyes and breathe out three times slowly. See yourself in a mirror as you are now. Looking into the mirror, go backward in time. Keep going back until you get to the time before you enlisted or before the trauma that changed you. See, sense, and feel yourself as you were then. Retrieve this image of yourself and become one with this self. Now go forward in time as this renewed self to the present. See yourself as you are to become in one year, three years, and five years. Breathe out and open your eyes.

> *Physical Exercise*: Hang a photo on a wall of yourself smiling taken prior to entering the military. Look at it once a day for 21 days.

CHAPTER 5

Anxiety and Fear

The constant watchfulness, or hypervigilance, required of combatants during war is critical to keep them safe. In modern warfare there are no battle lines; anyone can come under fire at any time. As a result, combatants never feel secure in the field, as they are on constant alert for danger. Danger can be an IED lying on the road, a missile launched at the field hospital, or a villager they were just talking to minutes ago suddenly going on the attack.

This constant watchfulness has two components — anxiety and fear. These feelings are intimately related, one feeding the other in a feedback loop. Fear is generated by an outside event or stimulus that happens in the present moment, while anxiety is about an unknown future. For example, if you are afraid of heights, you feel anxious before getting on the elevator that takes you to the top of the tower. Once in the elevator, you feel fear. Likewise, you may experience anxiety about going to sleep because you are afraid of having a nightmare. Once asleep and in a nightmare, you experience fear. The fear is what awakens you, causing your heart to pound and your skin to sweat profusely.

When you are chronically hyper-alert, you learn to live in a state of constant anxiety and fear. These rob you of normal rhythms of work and rest, which then interfere with your ability to think clearly. You come to believe that this hypervigilance keeps you safe from danger and that those who don't live this way are fools. Sadly, living in chronic states of anxiety means living in the future — always worried about what might happen at some future time. Anxiety robs you of living your life in the here and now, the only place of freedom.

So what do combatants do when, after two or three or four tours of duty, they find themselves back at home in the life they left a year or more ago, only to discover they aren't able to function like they used to? How can they reconcile seeing their family members and friends who never went to war lead lives where they casually go to the mall, walk down crowded sidewalks, drive in heavy traffic, and leave the front door unlocked as if these are safe activities? What do combatants do when they can't "turn off" their minds and relax?

❖

Paul was a Vietnam veteran who had just retired from a job with the Texas Border Patrol. For more than 30 years he had worked long hours, especially after he was promoted to supervisor. He had raised four daughters with his wife, Abigail, built his family a nice house, was thrilled when he became a grandfather, and was much loved by his extended family and friends.

He did okay, Paul said, until he retired at age 56. Suddenly,

Anxiety and Fear

with nothing to measure out his days, he had all this free time and "my mind began playing tricks on me." He started to think about his Vietnam war experiences "all the time," and then the nightmares started, and then not wanting to get together with the guys to play poker on Fridays, and eventually not wanting to leave the house "for any reason." Abigail begged him to accompany her on errands, but he wouldn't go. It got so bad he wouldn't even go to see their grandchildren.

When Paul went to the VA for his medical checkups, he could hardly bear the feelings that came over him. Paul described his visits like this: "First my mouth dries up, and then my heart starts to pound. Then I notice all the strangers sitting around me, and the clock on the wall starts to tick really loud." He said he felt so terrible that the only thing that would calm him would be to count the tiles on the floor. He just kept counting and counting until his name was called and he could go back to a private room and wait to see the doctor. He said that even though he knew that counting was "maybe not the best thing to do," he recognized that doing it in that circumstance soothed him. He was pleased that he had created a good coping strategy to get through a challenging situation. Building on that, I explained that in addition to distracting himself, he could also use his mind actively to clear out these old habits and ways of thinking.

After all, we can't let anything new in until we remove the clutter inside ourselves, be it fear, guilt, shame, or anger. In mental imagery, we can clean our bodies and our environment as well as our thoughts and feelings. Paul used **Clear Water** and **Stone of Fear** to clean out his anxiety and fear. Within two months, Paul was sleeping better, had mostly stopped thinking about his war experience, and was playing poker once more.

❖

Tanya had served three tours of duty on an aircraft carrier, and while she didn't experience direct combat, she had helped treat the many wounded who were evacuated to the ship at the beginning of the Gulf War. Even after all these years, she still couldn't sleep in her bed — she found she only felt secure sleeping on the floor with her head against the wall. This, of course, distressed her family.

When we met, she told me that she most wanted to change her sleep habits and to feel more relaxed at work and at home. I gave her the **Pendulum** exercise to do whenever she felt stressed or anxious. Next session, she reported that she was calmer all around. After several weeks she was able to sleep in bed and to manage her work and her family life with less anxiety.

IMAGERY EXERCISES FOR GENERAL ANXIETY

Pendulum

Intention: To remove anxiety.
Frequency: Morning, evening, and before bed for 21 days, and whenever you feel overcome with anxiety.

Anxiety and Fear

Close your eyes and breathe out three times slowly. See a pendulum that swings back and forth. On the right is the heap of your anxiety. See the pendulum swinging from the right, sweeping up some of the anxiety and taking it to the left. Then see the pendulum again swinging back to the right picking up some more of the anxiety and depositing it on the left.

The way to the right is now clearer and there is more freed space on the right, permitting the pendulum to swing even farther back to the right to pick up and carry away all the remaining anxiety to the left. As it does so, know that the anxiety is released. Now, see the pendulum swinging from the left in one great push to disperse the heap of anxiety straight up into the stratosphere until it has all disappeared. This causes a light rain to fall from a white cloud above you. Sense and feel this blessed rain cleansing and benefiting you. Breathe out and open your eyes.

> *Note:* Anytime you feel anxious, breathe out and for a few seconds see the pendulum swinging to the right to sweep the anxiety up and release it to the far left.

Clear Water

Intention: To detox yourself; to feel refreshed and renewed.
Frequency: Morning, evening, and before bed for 21 days.

Close your eyes and breathe out three times slowly. See yourself going to your kitchen, turning on the faucet, and filling a glass with clear water. Drink the water *slowly*, feeling it quenching your thirst and purifying you. After drinking the water, gently wash your hands and face with the clear running water. Feel that you are refreshed and renewed. Breathe out and open your eyes.

Stone of Fear

Intention: To get rid of fear.
Frequency: Morning, evening, and before bed for 21 days.

Close your eyes and breathe out three times slowly. See and sense the stone of fear lodged in your chest or throat. Reach your hands high up toward the sun, feeling the sun's warmth penetrating your hands and filling them with light. With your hands full of light, use your hands to gradually enlarge your throat and your chest. Place your hands of light into your chest or throat and carefully remove the stone, throwing it far behind you. Now very gently massage the area where the stone was lodged, bringing light and healing into the area. Breathe out and open your eyes.

Anxiety and Fear

The Room of Silence

Intention: To calm anxiety and reactivity to noises.
Frequency: Morning, evening, and before bed for 21 days.

Close your eyes and breathe out three times slowly. Imagine yourself in a room, noticing any noise. See a door to your right that leads into another room. Go through the door. If there is noise or cacophony, go through a door to your right, continuing in this way until you come to a *room of silence* where the noise has stopped. When you come to the room of silence, look around and see what you discover there. How do you feel? Breathe out and open your eyes.

> *Note:* When you first do this exercise, you may need to go through door after door until eventually you come to the room of silence, and when you do, the noise or anxiety is gone. What you see in the room of silence can serve as a reminder to shift into this room of silence whenever you feel anxious during your day.

Golden Net

Intention: To quell anxiety.
Frequency: Morning, evening, and before bed for 21 days.

Close your eyes and breathe out three times slowly. See, sense, and feel what anxiety looks like. Reeling it in with a golden net, put it into a deep cavern. Place a large rock at the mouth of the cavern, knowing that the anxiety is gone. Breathe out and open your eyes.

Sand Salutation

Intention: To feel refreshed, rejuvenated, and balanced.
Frequency: Once a day, upon arising in the morning, for 21 days.

Close your eyes and breathe out three times slowly. See, sense, and feel yourself stretched out on a beach, near the ocean. See the sun above you to the right. Feel the heat and light envelop you. Extending your arms toward the sun, catch its rays and bring the rays down to the center of your solar plexus (the area located between the end of your sternum/breastbone and your belly button).

Breathe out. Feel and sense the rays spreading from your solar plexus out to your entire body. See and feel these rays becoming increasingly blue, like the blue light that surrounds the sun and lights up the sky. These rays flow inside you like a long, calm river, spreading light within you. Feel yourself stimulated by this rush of life, full of peace and joy. Breathe out and open your eyes.

Anxiety and Fear

Emerald Dome

Intention: To calm yourself before going to sleep.
Frequency: Each night before going to sleep for 21 days, or as needed.

Close your eyes and breathe out three times slowly. See yourself enclosed in an emerald dome. See the glow of the emerald dome diffusing around you, filling you with its radiant light. Breathe out one time. Sense and feel this calming light protecting and shielding you from any disturbing feelings, thoughts, or sensations. Breathe out and open your eyes.

Staircases of Life

Intention: To relax and discover wholeness.
Frequency: Morning and evening for 21 days.

Close your eyes and breathe out three times slowly. Imagine yourself on the top floor of a house. See yourself descending down the back staircase of this house. At the bottom of the staircase, see, sense, and feel that you are perfect and whole just as you are. Know that all you may choose to be is already contained within you, ready to unfold. Breathe out one time. See, sense, and feel yourself ascending the front staircase and enter your special bedroom. Feel your body and mind relaxing as you lie down to rest and sleep, sensing your breath, rhythmic and even. Breathe out.

See, sense, and feel yourself awakening and refreshed. Breathe out and open your eyes.

CHAPTER 6

Anger

One of the cardinal symptoms of PTSD is anger. Anger can be a difficult feeling to deal with because it is socially unacceptable and can quickly spiral out of control, leading to dangerous situations for yourself or others. Perhaps more than with any other emotion, it is helpful to observe yourself in the moment of anger: What triggers it? What does the anger look like, feel like, and act like? For example, some people explode and direct the anger outward at others, while some shut down, become silent, and turn the anger inward. Anger can be expressed passively as sarcasm, apathy, or meanness, or actively through violent outbursts, scapegoating, and physical fighting. It can be experienced as anxiety and irritability as well. Anger is often reflected in our bodies as stomachaches, headaches, high blood pressure, chest tightening or heart palpitations, or fatigue.[3] No matter how we experience it, we want to actively take charge of the anger and curb it.

A Quick Way to Reverse Distressing Emotions

One easy way to change or reverse anger — or any distressing emotion — is to practice seeing (sensing and feeling) its opposite emotion. All language is based in opposites. You can't know light without knowing darkness; you can't know joy unless you know sorrow, etc. You can't know anger without knowing its opposite emotion. If you are asked to name the opposite of anger, you might say *calm*; others might say *feeling safe*, *secure*, or *peace*. Each of us can discover the opposite emotion for ourselves. And just as every word has an opposite, so does every word have a corresponding image. So if you were asked to see an image for *anger*, you might see a blazing fire while another person might imagine a volcano erupting. Likewise, you might see *calm* as a placid ocean while for another it might be a sleeping baby. Any image you see is correct.

Now that you know you can find the image for any distressing emotion, you can find its opposite by simply asking yourself what is the image of the distressing emotion and what is the image of its opposite. When the distressing emotion arises, you can then call to mind the opposite image by seeing, sensing, and feeling it for several seconds. For example, when you find yourself angry, you might see and sense a placid ocean. Your physiology will follow your images, and with practice (over 21 days or more) you will create new neural pathways that will diffuse the distressing emotion.

In addition to finding the opposite image, you can reverse a distressing emotion by "correcting" its corresponding image. For example, if you see anger as an exploding volcano, you might correct the image by seeing a strong rain shower dousing the flames.

When the distressing emotion arises, you can see (and sense and feel) this image of the rain shower for several seconds.

With anger (or any strong emotion), you can follow the rhythm of the emotion and do the imagery exercises at the moment the anger arises rather than just practicing at a set schedule of three times daily. At first, you will notice that many things trigger the anger, but over time, as you practice, you will begin to put a little wedge that grows bigger and bigger between the trigger and your habitual or automatic response to it so that the anger has less and less power over you. Remember not to berate yourself if you forget to do the exercise or if anger still overtakes you after doing the exercise.[4]

❖

Henry, a veteran of the war in Afghanistan, was sent to the Vet Center by the San Diego Veterans Court to get treatment for PTSD symptoms after he was arrested for assaulting a man in the parking lot of the local Home Depot. Henry believed that the man in question "stole my parking spot," so he waited until the man got out of his car and started yelling at him. A fistfight ensued, and the police were called. Even after he was handcuffed, he kept yelling obscenities at the man. It took two officers to get him into the squad car.

Once Henry arrived at the station and it was discovered that he was a recently returned veteran who had done four tours of combat duty, the police sergeant called Diane Parker, a defense attorney who works exclusively with veterans, to come down and interview him. Diane explained to Henry that there was a veteran's court so veterans could be treated for symptoms of PTSD instead of going to jail for minor infractions.

During the interview, Diane learned that Henry had been having serious symptoms of PTSD ever since his second deployment four years earlier. He had terrible nightmares and slept very little. He became extremely angry at the slightest provocation — so much so that he and his wife had separated a year ago because she became afraid of his explosive temper. He had lost his most recent job six months ago because everyone and everything made him angry. Now he spent his days shopping for materials for the home he was remodeling, but it was becoming more and more difficult because he was running into conflict with others almost every day.

Henry's relatives and colleagues had noticed that in addition to his anger he had become impatient, easily frustrated, and occasionally fearful. Anger had become his "go-to" response since he had returned from combat. The fighting response that had served him well in combat was making his life as a civilian a powder keg. Henry recognized this was the case, but he couldn't stop himself from exploding all too frequently. So we agreed to work together on anger management through various imagery exercises and the three magic breaths. After three months of practice, Henry said that he was less irritable, sleeping better, and able to catch himself before he exploded. His relationships with family and friends had improved, and he felt less wound up. In addition, he would often ask himself "Is this situation a true emergency?" This, he reported, helped him to calm down and respond appropriately when triggered as well.

IMAGERY EXERCISES DONE IN THE MOMENT OF ANGER

These exercises can be done with eyes open if necessary.

Blue Blood

Intention: To chill out and relax when you experience anger.
Frequency: Do this for 21 days, for several seconds, each time you experience anger.

Close your eyes and breathe out three times slowly. Imagine blue ice cubes on your temples and around your head. Sense the cool blue penetrating your skull, streaming down through your head, jaw, neck, chest, stomach, pelvis, legs, and feet, as well as your arms, hands, and fingers. Feel the anger and muscular tension dissipating as the cool blue stream flows out through the tips of your fingers and toes. Breathe out and open your eyes.

Noose of Anger

Intention: To relieve anger.
Frequency: Do for 21 days, for several seconds, each time you experience anger.

Close your eyes and breathe out three times slowly. Remove the noose that's constricting you. Sense and feel your body relaxing, your jaw loosening, and your breathing becoming deeper and slower. Breathe out and open your eyes, knowing that the anger is diminishing.

The Anger Speedometer

Intention: To gain control of your volatility, to stop automatic, hyper-reactive anger.
Frequency: Do for 21 days, for several seconds, each time you experience anger.

Close your eyes and breathe out three times slowly. Imagine a speedometer in front of you that measures your anger. See what your anger level is now, from 0 to 100. With your right hand, see, sense, and feel yourself lifting a handbrake that slowly reduces the speedometer until the point where you are calm. Breathe out one time. Notice the number on the speedometer now. Know that you can reduce the speedometer to this level of calm whenever you desire. Breathe out and open your eyes.

The Fireman's Hose

Intention: To cool down, to douse anger.
Frequency: Do for 21 days, for several seconds, each time you experience anger.

Close your eyes and breathe out three times slowly. See, sense, and feel your anger as a fire raging out of control. Take a fireman's hose and douse the fire with a strong stream of blue swirling water. When the fire is thoroughly doused, breathe out and open your eyes.

The Green Ball

Intention: To wash away anger.
Frequency: Do for 21 days, for several seconds, each time you experience anger.

Close your eyes and breathe out three times slowly. See, sense, and feel the anger as red ball of flame above your head. See this hot ball of fire turn into a cool green ball. As the ball breaks open, feel a cool green liquid washing down over you, from head to toe, leaving you feeling calm and relaxed. Breathe out and open your eyes.

Reversing Anger

Intention: To change anger to its opposite.
Frequency: Do for 21 days, for several seconds, each time you experience anger.

Close your eyes and breathe out three times slowly. See the image of anger. Now see its opposite image OR see an image that corrects or reverses the anger. Breathe out and open your eyes.

> *Note:* As you keep practicing this, you may find that you only need to recall in your mind's eye the opposite/corrected/reversed image for a second or two to regain your balance.

IMAGERY EXERCISES FOR ANGER PRACTICED THREE TIMES A DAY

Freed Prisoner

Intention: To master anger.
Frequency: Morning, evening, and before bed for 21 days.

Close your eyes and breathe out three times slowly. See a lion coming out of your mouth. He has been controlling you because you have been holding him prisoner. Now that you have freed him, you have become his master. Stroke him and tell him to leave you alone. Transfer his strength and life-energy to yourself. See that the parts of your body that have been suffering are now perfectly healed, strong, and light. See the vacant space that the lion has left in you. Fill it with whatever you want. When you no longer need the lion, let him leave freely. Watch him as he disappears. Breathe out and open your eyes, knowing that your anger is gone.

Remembering Love

Intention: To remember love.
Frequency: Morning, evening, and before bed for 21 days.

Close your eyes and breathe out three times slowly. Feel and live why a great sage said, "In anger you must remember love." Breathe out and open your eyes.

The Forest of Forgiveness

Intention: To forgive another.
Frequency: Morning and evening for 21 days.

Close your eyes and breathe out three times slowly. See yourself walking on a country road. You are dressed in white. Walking along, you come to a forest. Approaching the first line of trees surrounding the forest, you see the people who have caused you much pain, hurt, and grief emerging one by one from behind the trees. Breathe out. Identify each of these people and have them approach you one by one. Look them directly in the eye and tell each one what pain they have given you and ask them why. Hear their answer, and forgive each one. Send them on their way, knowing they are now behind you. Breathe out. Having a light with you, enter the forest, walking until you find a clearing in the forest's center. See the sun's rays beaming down, entering and penetrating you, cleansing and giving you strength. As you leave the forest to return to your chair, be aware of the fragrance of the flowers and the birds chirping. Breathe out and open your eyes.

> *Note:* As you do the exercise over a period of time, the people you encounter may change. You may find that as you forgive one, you open the channel for forgiveness in general. Also, you may come to see that anger is intimately connected to blaming another for your difficulties and/or their lacks. Here, you forgive them for being "imperfect beings." Finally, if you find yourself unable to forgive some, send them on their way, knowing that they are receding farther and farther from you, where they can no longer exert power over you.

Sitting Through Anger

Intention: To transform anger to its opposite.
Frequency: Morning, evening, and before bed for 21 days.

Close your eyes and breathe out three times slowly. See yourself sitting inside your anger. Find your way out and look at it. Decide what you want to do with it: transform it, dispose of it — it's your choice. Now see an opposite soothing image (such as sitting in the center of a rose or floating on a cloud). Breathe out and open your eyes, knowing that the anger is gone.

Anger

> *Note:* It's best to find your own images directly from your own experience.

PHYSICAL EXERCISES FOR ANGER

1. Find or purchase a green or blue stone. Carry this stone in your pocket. Whenever you experience anger, touch the stone, knowing that the anger is lessening. Sense your breathing slowing down, your chest and abdomen expanding with each exhalation, and your jaw relaxing.
2. Wear an amulet of your choice, such as a cross, star of David, the eye of Horus, hamsa, or an ankh. Touch the amulet, knowing that it is absorbing the anger.
3. Carry an essential oil with a fragrance that soothes you, such as lavender, sandalwood, bergamot, geranium, or jasmine. Smell it each time you feel anger arising.

CHAPTER 7

Triggers

As we have seen, one of the most common residual responses to having been in combat is hypervigilance. As we saw with Mr. James, all of these things can be made worse by triggers, meaning that a person responds in an exaggerated way to an "ordinary" experience that would not have upset them before the traumatic event. Although the trigger itself need not be frightening or traumatic, it indirectly or superficially is reminiscent of an earlier traumatic incident. I have seen first Gulf War veterans triggered by wildfires (fire reminds them of the burning oil wells), Vietnam veterans triggered by the sound of helicopters, Korean war veterans triggered by extreme cold (many didn't have enough warm clothing in the brutal winters and suffered from frostbite). Add to these sudden noises, smells of ethnic foods cooking, and other everyday occurrences, and it is clear that triggers are hard to avoid.

Sean is a Vietnam vet who is attending an evening class at the Vet Center. We are in a circle introducing ourselves at the start of

Triggers

the first class. Suddenly Sean jumps up and without a word strides out of the room and doesn't return that evening. The following week he arrives early to the class and explains that he had smelled Vietnamese food being warmed up in the adjacent kitchen and was suddenly overcome with anxiety; he felt he was back in the war.

❖

Jenny lives in an apartment on the second floor of a four-plex at the end of a cul-de-sac. It only has one door, on which Jenny has installed three locks. From the two picture windows in the living/dining room, she can see 180 degrees all the way down the street and to the left and right of the property. Any noise from residents, delivery trucks, or even children playing in the park across the street makes her jump. She has become so skittish that she now sleeps on the sofa in front of the door so she can get up quickly and look out her windows if there is any noise during the night.

After doing one or more of the following imagery exercises, both these veterans have made improvements in the way they cope with life. Jenny has stopped needing to check her door locks throughout the night and can get some sleep; she has made a commitment to come into town and visit her family once a week, and she uses the breathing exercises to help her if she gets anxious. By working on his general anxiety problems, Sean can tolerate smells that would otherwise have set him off.

Below are imagery exercises for social gatherings, smells, driving, and sound triggers. You are most likely to encounter these triggers while you are out and about, but even if you can't sit in a chair with your eyes closed, you can still do the exercises with open eyes for a moment.

IMAGERY EXERCISES TO FEEL SAFE

Un-triggering Yourself

Intention: To feel safe in social gatherings and events.
Frequency: Morning, evening, and before bed for 21 days, and before social gatherings.

Close your eyes and breathe out three times. See, sense, and feel yourself calmly preparing for the upcoming social situation (family gathering, party, church, business interview). Breathe out one time. Now, see yourself entering the gathering, and find a place within this group where you feel comfortable and at ease, having with you whatever or whomever you need to feel safe. Know that you are free to leave and to return whenever you want. Breathe out one time and open your eyes.

My Sweet Heaven

Intention: To create a safe haven.
Frequency: Do this exercise for 21 days whenever you find yourself feeling panicked, anxious, or pressured, responding to a false emergency.

Close your eyes and breathe out three times slowly. Imagine you are building a sanctuary for yourself, a place where you feel at home, safe, and content. By your side are materials you need to build this structure. After you've constructed your sanctuary, step inside and look around, decorating and furnishing it as you wish. Know that this sanctuary is always available to you. Breathe out and open your eyes.

Note: You build your safe space the first time you do this exercise. After that you can return to it imaginally, with eyes open or closed, for several seconds whenever you feel uncomfortable or unsafe.

As you practice, you may find that you catch yourself earlier and earlier from responding to the false emergency.

IMAGERY FOR SMELL TRIGGERS

Life Can Be a Bed of Roses

Intention: To eliminate your response to the triggering smell.
Frequency: Use whenever you are upset by a smell.

Close your eyes and breathe out three times slowly. See yourself lying in a huge bed of fragrant rose petals, inhaling their smell and feeling at ease. Breathe out and open your eyes.

The Tree of Life

Intention: To eliminate your response to the triggering smell.
Frequency: Use whenever triggered.

With eyes either opened or closed, see yourself leaning back against a large tree that has abundant leaves, breathing in the pure oxygen as blue-golden light and exhaling any toxins and carbon dioxide as gray smoke that drifts far away from you. Feel the calm energy of the tree penetrating and soothing you. Breathe out and open your eyes.

PHYSICAL EXERCISES FOR TRIGGERING SMELLS

Scents

Go to your bathroom, kitchen cabinet, or a natural foods store that carries essential oils or herbs. Find a scent you like (such as an herbal tea bag, vanilla extract, lavender, peppermint, cinnamon, cardamom, anise, lemon, or freshly ground coffee beans). Carry a small sample with you and smell it anytime you are triggered by a distressing odor, knowing that as you inhale the pleasant scent, you feel calmed and centered.

IMAGERY FOR DRIVING TRIGGERS

The Chariot

Intention: To remain centered and calm while driving.
Frequency: Morning, evening, and before bed for 21 days. Do this exercise just before driving as well. As with all imagery exercises, you can repeat the exercise for another two cycles of 21 days, stopping seven days between cycles.

Close your eyes and breathe out three times. Become a superhero who wears golden armor, standing in a golden chariot pulled by winged horses. Have with you all that you need to accomplish your mission. Breathe out one time. Gather up all who need to be rescued and clothe them in suits of protective golden armor. See the winged horses leading the chariot to safety. Remove your armor and sense yourself breathing freely and unconstricted. Breathe out and open your eyes.

> *Note:* If you find yourself becoming anxious or worried while driving, take three quieting breaths. Then, WITH EYES OPEN, staying alert to the traffic, for just a moment see in your mind's eye the image of the chariot soaring above the ground. This mini image will act as a reminder to remain calm and balanced.

The Red Sea Parting/Safe Passage
- See page 30 -

IMAGERY EXERCISES FOR NOISE TRIGGERS

Cheering from the Stands

Intention: To drown out unpleasant sounds.
Frequency: Use whenever triggered.

Close your eyes and breathe out three times slowly. See yourself back in time at your favorite ball game or athletic event. See yourself cheering with the roar of the crowd as your team wins the game. Breathe out and open your eyes, knowing that you are on the winning team.

Melody of Life

Intention: To replace the triggering noise with a more pleasant sound. This exercise can also be used to ease feelings of isolation.
Frequency: Use whenever triggered.

Close your eyes and breathe out three times slowly. See yourself at a concert by your favorite music band or orchestra, cheering and singing along with the crowd, feeling joyful. Breathe out and open your eyes, keeping this feeling of joy with you.

The Room of Silence
- See page 41 -

Helicopter Trigger Exercise
(Especially for Vietnam veterans)

Intention: To desensitize yourself to helicopter sounds.
Frequency: Morning, evening, and before bed for 21 days. In addition, whenever you are triggered by a helicopter sound, see the corrected image for a few seconds.

Close your eyes and breathe out three times. Become a superhero warrior in a golden chariot drawn by winged horses. See yourself having with you all that you need to accomplish this mission. Breathe out one time. See yourself gathering up all who need to be rescued and clothe them in suits of golden armor. See the chariot returning to safety. Remove your armor, sensing yourself breathing more freely and unconstricted. With each in breath, feel your lungs filling with air, sensing your ribs, chest, and abdomen expanding. With each out breath, feel and sense everything contracting and relaxing. Then, breathe out and open your eyes.

CHAPTER 8

Isolation

After years of not being sure who is friend and who is enemy, it is not easy to once again trust strangers. Combat veterans often err on the side of caution; still on guard, they trust no one and are always looking over their shoulders, just in case. They wonder how their family members can be so easygoing and lose faith in their family's competence. Pretty soon the internal conflict of war expands to a conflict between themselves and their family and friends. They begin to withdraw, feeling they can only trust themselves.

Many combatants and veterans isolate themselves. They start turning down all invitations from family and friends because it is just easier to be alone at home. At the ballpark there are too many crowds, at the barbecue there are too many little kids running around, at the movies a gunman might easily come in from behind and the moviegoers are just sitting ducks. Soon the invitations stop coming and the combatants/veterans are alone, or alone within their immediate families. Their families feel hurt and oftentimes resentful because the veterans don't want to participate in communal activities.

Reversing the Trauma of War

❖

Sarah can't bear to be with people, not even her own family. She has moved several miles out of town to a remote cabin on top of a hill that can only be reached by a dirt road. Her Jeep has been caught in the mud several times when it rains, but she doesn't care. She got two German shepherds that she has trained as guard dogs and found a job she can do from home. Once a week, her sister comes for dinner and brings groceries so Sarah will have enough to eat for the week.

❖

Roy, a 30-year-old, had been in the army and completed four tours of duty in Iraq before he was discharged for severe symptoms of war trauma. His family had insisted he come to the Center for treatment because of his increasing isolation. He would not join the family even for meals and never ventured out — he preferred to stay in his room, where he felt safe and in control. He chose to sleep during the day, when he could easily check for intruders if he heard any unfamiliar sounds. At night, he stayed outside the house, patrolling the property perimeter as well as gardening and pruning trees so he could maintain clear lines of vision. When I met him two years after his return to the States, he was clearly suffering with severe symptoms of PTSD: hypervigilance, disturbed sleep habits, and isolation. Over several months, we worked on this mosaic of symptoms. Using the cocoon and perimeter-check exercises in conjunction with sleeping medication, Roy became able to join the family for meals, work locally at gardening jobs, go to the movies, and grocery shop.

IMAGERY EXERCISES FOR ISOLATION

Coming Out of the Shadows

Intention: To feel comfortable and at ease around people.
Frequency: Morning, evening, and before bed for 21 days.

Close your eyes and breathe out three times slowly (or take several rounds of quieting breaths, breathing in blue-gold light and breathing out gray smoke). See yourself engulfed in shadows. How do you feel? Breathe out one time and see yourself emerging out of the shadows and into the light. See, sense, and feel the light cascading down over you and filling you. What do you experience and discover? Breathe out and open your eyes.

The Cocoon

Intention: To come out of isolation.
Frequency: Morning, evening, and before bed for 21 days.

Close your eyes and breathe out three times slowly. See, sense, and feel yourself wrapped within a silk cocoon. Sense the walls surrounding you, keeping you safe while you grow and transform.

Breathe out one time. Feel your arms growing very, very long. As you stretch your limbs, sense the cocoon thinning until you push through the wall of the cocoon, breaking through into the light of the sun. Then, step out of the cocoon knowing that you are free. Look around to see what you discover. Breathe out and open your eyes.

The Guest House

Intention: To come out of isolation.
Frequency: Morning, evening, and before bed for 21 days.

Close your eyes and breathe out three times slowly. See, sense, and feel yourself as a guest house. Every morning a new guest arrives on your doorstep. Breathe out one time. Feel joy knocking at your door. Breathe out one time. Feel sadness as it creeps in. Breathe out one time. Sense how anger abruptly takes over. Breathe out one time. Become aware of how these feelings come and go, arise and disappear.

Breathe out one time. Now greet these guests with laughter, no matter who they may be — dark thoughts, shame, or malice. Know that they are only passing through the front door and exiting through the back door — if you let them. Breathe out and open your eyes.

CHAPTER 9

Depression

> Note: Veterans, like many others, have passing thoughts, feelings, and images of suicide. If at any time you feel that you want to harm yourself, this is an emergency and should be treated as such. Go directly to the nearest emergency room, either at a veterans' hospital or any community hospital. If possible, have a family member or friend go with you. The Veterans Crisis hotline is a 24-hour free and confidential service available to all veterans and families. You can expect knowledgeable, experienced veterans and VA therapists to caringly, compassionately "be there for you." You are NEVER alone. Reach out for help. You can reach the hotline in any of these ways:
>
> - Call 1-800-273-TALK, then press #1
> - Text to 838255
> - Chat confidentially online at www.veteranscrisisline.net
> - TTY service available at 1-800-799-4889.

Depression takes many forms for those with PTSD: sadness, moodiness, grief, mourning, despair, and distress are some of these. Symptoms of depression also include sleep problems, lethargy, loss of interest in things you used to enjoy, loss of appetite, and inability to concentrate.

Veterans/combatants who are depressed have a tendency to self-medicate, which can take the form of alcohol or drug use. Often after some months, it takes more and more of the substance to get the same effect. Veterans find that they are dependent and spiraling out of control. Then they have *two* problems — a mood disorder and a drug problem. The latter generally contributes to the mood disorder becoming more pronounced, since alcohol and many other drugs are depressants.

❖

Rob was an Operation Iraqi Freedom veteran who had done three tours of duty in Iraq and had returned to civilian life five years earlier. The first time I saw him he explained why he came to see me: "My girlfriend said either I come see you or the relationship is over. I really love her and want to make this work, so here I am."

He described a fight they had had a few nights before. He had become so enraged that he'd put his fist through the wall, and then he tore the door off the kitchen cabinet. "She was really scared, even though I would never, ever hit her. Even *I* was scared. I don't know where this rage came from, and worse than that, I felt so sad. The truth is, I feel really sad a lot of the time these days…."

Depression

"You know," I said, "anger is often the flip side of depression."

I asked him to tell me about a typical day. He was a full-time student and also worked part-time, so he was always feeling the pressure of time, and that, he said, "stresses me out." He was getting straight A's in his business classes and intended to go on for an MBA. His girlfriend had a small son, so he was involved in parenting duties at home. By the end of what was usually a 12- to 14-hour day, he was so keyed up that the only way he found to calm himself was to drink a couple of beers when he got home. "But what's happened," he said, "is that two beers turned into four and those turned into six. Now it takes a six-pack to do what a drink or two would have done a year ago. And I still can't relax, and that means I can't get much sleep."

We talked about symptoms of depression: feeling on edge; difficulty concentrating; fatigue and decreased energy; insomnia; early-morning wakefulness or excessive sleeping; irritability; loss of interest in activities once pleasurable; feelings of hopelessness; feelings of guilt, worthlessness, and/or helplessness; and thoughts of death and dying. We discussed the feeling of being out of control and taking those feelings out on the people we live with and love.

"That sounds like a picture of me, Doc," he said. "How can we fix it?"

We discussed the importance of being assessed for clinical depression, because such severe depression often leads to thoughts and feelings of suicide. Such thoughts must be professionally assessed so that veterans/combatants can be helped to understand and cope with their depression.

After he was assessed, it was clear that Rob was not clinically depressed, so we began to do exercises that would help him to manage his mood by getting unstuck, physically, emotionally, and mentally. After we had worked together for four months, Rob was able to overcome the depression, and later he told me that he married his girlfriend and went on to graduate school.

IMAGERY EXERCISES FOR DEPRESSION

Blowing Away the Dark Clouds

Intention: To lift depression.
Frequency: Morning, evening, and before bed for 21 days.

Close your eyes and breathe out three times slowly. See dark gray clouds above you. Imaginally, blow the clouds away to your left with three strong breaths. After you have blown away the clouds, look to the upper right and see the sun rising. Watch it move to the center of your vision, replacing the dark clouds. Know and feel the depression lifting as you look to your upper right. Breathe out and open your eyes.

> *Note:* Generally, in imagery the right signifies the future, the left signifies the past.

The Black Hole

Intention: To overcome depression and despair.
Frequency: Morning, evening, and before bed for 21 days.

Close your eyes and breathe out three times. Imagine yourself in a black hole. Have with you a flashlight and, looking around, find anything that you need to help you climb out of the hole. Sense and feel that the depression is lifting with each step of your ascent. Breathe out. When you reach the top, step out of the hole. What do you see and feel? Know that the depression is lifted. Breathe out and open your eyes.

SWALLOWING THE RAINBOW

Intention: To relieve depression connected with feelings of hopelessness and isolation or for internal mood shifts *not* connected to outside circumstances.
Frequency: Morning, evening, and before bed for 21 days.

Close your eyes and breathe out three times slowly. Imagine swallowing a rainbow. What do you sense and feel? Stay with this feeling for a few seconds. Breathe out and open your eyes.

The Blue Sky Umbrella

Intention: To lift despair and create protection.
Frequency: Morning, evening, and before bed for 21 days, and whenever you feel overcome with despair.

Close your eyes and breathe out three times slowly. Imagine you have an oversized umbrella. Open the umbrella and see that it covers you with a cloudless, bright-blue sky that extends outward in all directions, covering and protecting you and your loved ones. Breathe out and open your eyes.

The Drop of Hope
(Two exercises done together)

Intention: To transform despair to hope.
Frequency: Morning, evening, and before bed for 21 days.

1. Close your eyes and breathe out three times slowly. Imagine yourself holding a glass of clear, pure water. See and hear the descent of a drop of ink and the rhythm and ripple patterns of the water. Hear what the water is saying to you when it has been hurt or disturbed by the black drop. What are you feeling? Live these feelings deeply by allowing them to fill you. Then wash yourself out by (imaginally) drinking a glass of clear, pure water. Breathe out and open your eyes, knowing that the despair has lifted.

Depression

2. Close your eyes and breathe out three times slowly. Let fall a drop of heavy white ink into the clear, pure water. Look at how far it goes down into the water. See and hear the descent of the drop and the rhythm and ripple patterns of the water. Hear what the water is saying to you when it has been hurt or disturbed by the white drop. What are you feeling? Live these feelings deeply by allowing them to fill you. Breathe out and open your eyes, knowing that the despair has lifted.

Ra

Intention: To overcome depression or addiction, and to be born anew.
Frequency: Morning, evening, and before bed for 21 days.

Close your eyes and breathe out three times. See, feel, and sense yourself as a swallow flying up the ladder to heaven. Sit in the hands of the Egyptian sun god Ra (or, if you prefer, sit in God's hand). He buries you in the blue egg of the world. Breathe out. Feel and sense yourself pressed into the soil. Now, begin rising, becoming a new person, growing toward the sun. Then breathe out and open your eyes.

Deep Cleansing from Childhood

Intention: To clean out troubling memories and feelings.
Frequency: Do this exercise in the morning, upon awakening, for seven days.

Close your eyes and breathe out three times slowly. Carefully watch for the strategies you use to maintain your identity that you developed by age 4. Breathe out. Know what has made you the person you are now.

Breathe out. See the two most significant events in your life. See that these images reveal yourself as you have been in the past and as you are now. Breathe out. Return to your childhood at age 4 or 5. See the disturbing emotions you felt and the places, events, and people connected with these emotions. With your left hand, take a golden brush or cloth and wipe these feelings and events away to the far left.

Breathe out. See, sense, and feel how you have the power to change your emotions and memories. Breathe out and open your eyes.

PHYSICAL EXERCISES FOR DEPRESSION

Clothing Choice

Each day, put on a brightly colored garment or accessory (hat, cap, socks, scarf, bracelet, ties) of red, yellow, or orange to remind you of the possibility of a new mood. Avoid wearing dark clothing, including black, even if at first this seems difficult for you. (Never mind if you don't like any of these colors. Wearing a color you dislike creates balance within you).

> *Note*: If you are active duty military, then follow this when you are off duty.

Mirror Exercise

Hang a mirror by the inner entrance of your home or room (or, if not possible, set a mirror on a table). At the start of your day, look at yourself in this mirror and smile for a moment before you leave home.

Drawing Spirals

Spirals, unlike circles, are open-ended systems of movement that permit growth. Spirals abound in our biology and in nature — for example, in our fingerprints, our DNA, in sea shells, sunflowers, snails, elephant trunks, etc.

On a drawing pad or tablet, use a pencil to draw a spiral from inside growing out in a clockwise direction.

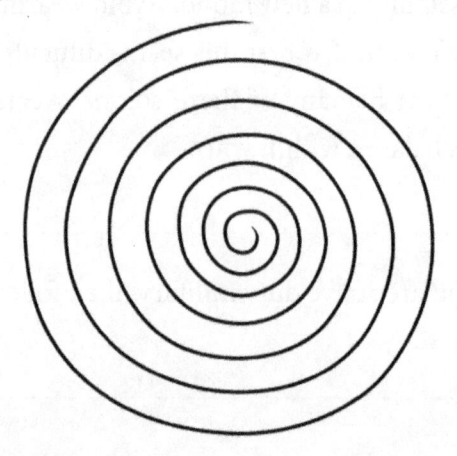

With each turn of the spiral, feel yourself become more energized, focused, and calm. Do this when you are feeling down, for 30 seconds to a minute.

Clean a Space

Each morning, physically clean a small area of your home — a sink, mirror, window, floor, desk, etc. Do it with the intention of cleaning out the gloom, depression, fatigue, or sadness you feel.

CHAPTER 10

Guilt

Bill was a 31-year-old sergeant who had considered being a soldier as a lifetime profession before his second tour of duty in Iraq. All that changed on a dark October evening in a small village where he and his men were going house-to-house looking for suspected insurgents. Just before they got to the last house, a young boy ran in front of them and threw a grenade, and just as it exploded, rapid gunfire erupted from the house, only about 20 yards from their position. Everyone hit the ground, but it was no use — they were outnumbered and unable to reach for their weapons, as most of the men had been gravely wounded during the grenade blast.

When the rest of the unit arrived as backup, Bill was the only soldier alive. He had lost five men, men he had trained and grown to love like brothers. He didn't even want to live but had no choice, as he was carried to a waiting truck and whisked away to a field hospital.

It took eight months to recuperate back at The Walter Reed National Military Medical Center in Washington, D.C. During that whole time, Bill said he woke up every morning wishing he were dead, and the feeling didn't go away once he was discharged and moved back home.

Bill described in detail how he and his wife moved to a ranch that lay right on the border between California and Mexico. He explained that he had joined a group of vigilantes who patrolled the border, and for the past couple of years, he had been out most nights looking for illegal aliens who came through his property. Last week, he had found a group of people with their coyote, and there had been an exchange of gunfire (Bill was always armed). When the border patrol arrived on the scene, they were horrified to see that Bill was shooting without taking cover, making himself a target. They told him that if he didn't go get help for this "crazy" behavior, they were going to arrest him. That's how he came to be in my office.

"Well," I said to him, "it looks like you're trying to commit suicide by having the law shoot you down in a gunfight."

"Yeah," he said. "Doesn't much matter to me if I live or die."

"Does it matter to your wife and kids?"

"Well, yeah, of course." He stroked his beard. "Never thought of it that way."

"What are you so depressed about that you want to die?" I asked him.

He was quiet for a minute. Then his eyes filled with tears. "Six years ago in Ramadi, I lost all my men. It was my fault. I don't deserve to go on living."

"During wartime we confront terrorists; the enemy is external," I said. "In the work we are doing here, we are confronting the terrorists that have now become inner terrorists. Our aim is for

Guilt

you to conquer these inner terrorists, to overcome them. That's what you have control of.

"Living with guilt means you have given power to the past, and that is the controlling issue of your life right now. What we are working toward here is freedom. To get there, you need to pay attention to what is happening in the moment. That is the only rule."

Next, I explained to Bill that there is a difference between guilt, remorse, and regret. Guilt is a debt you feel you owe to someone. Remorse is the bad feeling you have after an event. Regret is to feel sad or sorry about something you did or did not do.

I explained that in order to be in the moment, it's important not to make judgments about what happened or should have happened, or about what we should be feeling now. Just keep looking at the facts, not the added judgments about the facts. What is in front of you now? You are here, present in this moment. You are not at war. There is no gun to your head. What do you see in *this* present moment? *You always have a choice*. You can retrain yourself not to shift into the past or the future; you can learn to stay present.

I explained to him, "It is possible to honor the dead without making yourself a martyr. It is possible to honor them in the most time-honored way — to live, as the survivor, a good life, a life of meaning."

Bill was able to see the damage his way of thinking was doing to his life, and especially to his family's life. He set to work doing the following imagery exercises and saw me every week while doing so. After several months of practicing mental imagery exercises, Bill gained more control over his behavior and actions, and most significantly, he recognized how important he was to his family's well-being.

> ## To Recap
>
> We retrain ourselves to live in the moment:
> - By actively recognizing when we have strayed out of the present and into the past or future;
>
> - By breathing out three times when we feel overwhelmed by guilt and anxiety;
>
> - By doing mental imagery exercises to help us let go of the memories of the past (i.e., the actual events or "facts" and our judgments about what happened, should have happened, or might happen);
>
> - By making any reparations — through mental imagery and through physical acts of service.

IMAGERY EXERCISES FOR GUILT

Red Ribbon

Intention: To eliminate guilt feelings.
Frequency: Each morning for seven, 14, or 21 days.

Close your eyes and breathe out three times slowly. See a red ribbon in front of you. Write on this ribbon the traits and feelings you want to be rid of, including guilt. List these traits in the order of importance they hold for you. Put the ribbon around your neck.

Breathe out once and go from the city into a desert. Find yourself at the base of a waterfall that has a large rock nearby. Dig a hole in front of the rock. Take all the traits from the ribbon and expel them one by one by breathing out each time you name a trait (not out loud, but imaginally to yourself there in the desert). Afterward, place the ribbon on the rock and burn it. Place the ashes into the hole you dug, filling in the hole, placing the rock on top of it. Breathe out and go to the waterfall. Climb from the bottom to the top, straight up the cascading water itself. See, sense and feel the force of the water rushing over you, cleansing you, and washing away any residual guilt. Breathe out one time, and come out of the waterfall. Let the sun dry you. Put on a clean robe or gown, knowing your guilt is gone. Breathe out and open your eyes.

The Jail of Guilt

Intention: To free yourself.
Frequency: Once in the morning for 21 days.

Close your eyes and breathe out three times slowly. Imagine that you are in a jail. Have a light with you. Look around and find the key to unlock the cell door. Unlock the door and leave, taking the key with you.

Approach the guard and tell him you are leaving. See him nod yes. Thank him and walk beyond him to a staircase that has three *tall* steps. Climb these steps *slowly*. At the top, find a door, open it and walk out, and close the door behind you. What do you discover and how do you feel? Breathe out and open your eyes.

> *Note:* If the jailer objects, know that you can return to the cell and lock yourself back in, keeping the key for future use when you are ready to free yourself. If you discover that you owe something to someone (living or dead), pay the debt either by making amends to the person directly or by giving charity in the person's name or some similar act.

Guilt

Take Me to the River

Intention: To be reborn; to be free of guilt.
Frequency: Twice a day, upon awakening in the morning and before bed, for 21 days.

Close your eyes and breathe out three times slowly. Imagine yourself on the banks of the River Jordan. See Jesus (or any meaningful spiritual teacher or healer) by your side. Remove all your clothing and with Jesus leading you by the hand, walk into the water until you are shoulder deep. Breathe out. Submerge yourself in the water, asking forgiveness of anyone, living or dead, you have harmed. Come up knowing they have forgiven you. Breathe out. Submerge yourself once again in the water, asking forgiveness of God for any harm you feel you have caused. Come up, knowing you have been forgiven. Breathe out. Submerge yourself a third time, asking *yourself* for forgiveness. Come up knowing that you have repented in your heart. Return to the shore and find clean clothes on the banks. Put them on, knowing you are reborn and freed of guilt. Breathe out and open your eyes.

❖

Repentance is a necessary step in letting go of guilt. To repent means both to regret (in French) and to return (in Hebrew). With imagery, we make a new turn toward life, health, and wholeness by acknowledging our errors and then correcting them.

Repentance: Reversing Errors of the Past

Intention: To repent and let go of our mistakes and errors.
Frequency: Once a year.

Close your eyes and breathe out three times slowly. See yourself traveling on the back of a dragon. See yourself ascending with the dragon through the stages of your development as you fly from inside the earth to the highest mountain and from cloud to cloud above the seven skies; then see yourself returning to earth.

Breathe out one time. See and sense the Archangel Raphael, the angel of healing, standing behind you.

Breathe out one time and do an examination of conscience, beginning from the present moment and going backward in time to your earliest childhood, and identify disturbing memories and events. See how doing this helps you recognize the pain you have caused yourself and others.

Breathe out SLOWLY one time and repair any damage you have done to others, dead or alive. Ask for forgiveness from those you have offended, humiliated, or abused.

Breathe out SLOWLY one time and discover the guilts that bring you feelings of shame and regret.

Breathe out SLOWLY one time and repent the evil done in the past, beginning from now back to your conception.

Breathe out SLOWLY one time and repent honestly with all your heart.

Breathe out and sense a new well-being filling you, as you return from the time of conception to now, cleansed and renewed.

Breathe out one time. See that by repenting, you are reaching the *now*, no longer blaming others or yourself. See a river flowing through you, cleansing you. Breathe out and open your eyes.

IMAGINAL MIRROR EXERCISES

We use mirrors in our everyday life to get the "whole picture" — for example, when we groom ourselves each morning, or look through the car's rearview mirror when driving. Likewise, when we hold up one hand to a mirror, the reflection is of the other hand. The mirror offers back a reverse image of our hand that completes our experience of handedness — for we now have two hands! In a sense, when looking in a mirror, we can experience our own wholeness.

The image in the mirror has form but no physical substance. Through the ages, people have understood the mirror to be a portal and access point between the physical, concrete reality and other levels of reality. For example, in the *Snow White* fairy tale, the queen's magical mirror provides answers and speaks the truth. Likewise, in *Alice in Wonderland,* Alice goes through the looking glass (a mirror) to journey into her inner subjective reality, where she discovers an entire world. Mirrors are the perfect "reversing" devices to help bring about change. We too can use imaginal mirrors to help ourselves see the whole picture, see the truth of the matter, and envision new possibilities.

Replacing the Bad with the Good

Intention: To let go of guilt and anxiety
Frequency: Morning, evening, and before bed for eight days. Practice only one exercise a day, then move on to the next exercise the following day.

Day 1 Close your eyes and breathe out three times slowly. Look into a mirror and see evil and guilt. See yourself refusing to accept the evil and guilt. Using your left hand, wipe away the images to the left, out of the mirror. Turn the mirror over, and see that good appears in place of evil and guilt. Keep this good feeling for yourself, assured that everything is coming into order. Breathe out and open your eyes.

Day 2 Close your eyes and breathe out three times slowly. Looking into a mirror, see yourself climbing up a ladder high above the clouds. What are you feeling? Breathe out and open your eyes.

Day 3 Close your eyes and breathe out three times slowly. Looking into a mirror, see yourself refusing to throw out the baby with the bathwater. Breathe out and open your eyes.

Day 4 Close your eyes and breathe out three times slowly. Looking into a mirror, see yourself sifting the chaff from the wheat, noticing that some seeds are beginning to grow out of the discarded chaff. Breathe out and open your eyes.

Day 5 Close your eyes and breathe out three times slowly. Looking into a mirror, see yourself wearing boots that are so

Guilt

heavy that you cannot move your legs. Now, see yourself wearing normal shoes, and then wearing very light sandals that allow you to fly over the embers of a fire that is in front of you. Breathe out and open your eyes.

Day 6 Close your eyes and breathe out three times slowly. Looking into a mirror, see someone losing the ground under their feet. See them somersaulting or falling straight down, landing on their feet, and walking with their family into a clear, large, calm space. What do you now feel guilty about? To what standards are you holding yourself? Breathe out and open your eyes.

Day 7 Close your eyes and breathe out three times slowly. Looking into a mirror, see and know that only what you can accept can come to you, delivered to your all-knowing mind. See, observe, and accept only what you decide is good for you. Breathe out and open your eyes.

Day 8 Close your eyes and breathe out three times slowly. Imagine a mirror in which you are seeing yourself winning the upper hand. Then see yourself with an axe in your hand. Throw the blade, then the handle, into the mirror, pushing them away to the left, out of the mirror. Now turn the mirror over and see yourself:

1) Casting away sadness and guilt.
2) Repairing the axe by putting together the handle and the blade.

Looking into the mirror, see yourself smiling, creating the qualities of health and assuredness. With your right hand, push this image to the right, out of the mirror. Breathe out and open your eyes.

The War Within

Intention: Getting rid of undesirable traits.
Frequency: Morning, evening, and before bed for 21 days.

Close your eyes and breathe out three times slowly. Imagine a mirror; see in it an undesirable habit. Then turn the mirror over and see the undesirable habit turned into a desirable habit.

Breathe out slowly one time. See yourself as the all-knowing One. Look at all the undesirable traits of the past, starting from now and going back in time. See how each of these traits will be lived out in the future if not changed now.

Breathe out slowly one time. Looking into the mirror, see yourself at the seashore, emptying your pockets. Breathe out each distressing trait into the clear, vast space of sky and ocean.

Breathe out slowly one time. With one foot in the sea and one on shore, take a large ram's horn, blowing it into the clear light. Sense and feel the light and sound resounding and reverberating within you. On the shore, find a light suit or cloak and put it on. Feel and know that by truly knowing — and accepting — what you are, all errors cease. Breathe out and open your eyes.

CHAPTER 11

Insomnia and Nightmares

One of the most common complaints of combatants and veterans are sleep-related disorders such as insomnia, nightmares, and acting out physically while still asleep, which is called night terrors. There are many reasons for sleep disturbance: Training for war includes sleep-disturbing routines such as sentry duty and watch; the nature of combat means often being interrupted during sleep by incoming fire or other disturbances; and many of the medications prescribed to warriors have four-hour cycles. These altered sleep rhythms combine with anxiety, hypervigilance, and chronic pain syndromes to create sleepless nights. No wonder combatants often have trouble falling asleep, staying asleep, or both.

Insomnia and Pain

Often when pain wakes us up from a sound sleep, we will not be able to get back to sleep. Without enough rest, many of the other symptoms of PTSD are exacerbated, and we find ourselves caught in a vicious downward spiral.

Adrienne had been a reservist who never thought she would see action in combat. She had been in the Army as a young woman but left when she married and had a child. Now, at 37, she was an Army reservist who had just returned from six months in Afghanistan, where she had seen a great deal of action. She was a driver, and she drove many convoys through the mountains from one base to another.

She carried equipment in her truck so she could tow away disabled vehicles, and more than once, she had to inspect a vehicle that had blown up and still contained body parts. During her two tours of duty, she had hurt her back, suffered traumatic brain injury (TBI) in a huge explosion, broken her leg, and started to get headaches due to the constant ringing in her ears. She had just received a 70 percent service-connected disability rating.

"But I want to work," she said. She had just finished her degree in engineering and had been hired by the county as a structural engineer. "My family needs the money," she explained, "and I need to keep doing something that has meaning for me. Please help me to deal with this pain so I don't have to take so many mind-numbing drugs."

She stayed on her drug regimen while we began doing the pain exercises found in Chapter 13 and **The Setting Sun** exercise below to ease her into sleep. Within two months, she was able to cut her medication dose by half (after consulting with her physician) and could function well in both her personal and professional life.

Insomnia and Nightmares

IMAGERY EXERCISES FOR INSOMNIA

The Setting Sun

Intention: To fall asleep easily and peacefully.
Frequency: Each night before bed for 21 days or as needed. If you become reliant or habituated to it, take a break for seven days, choose another exercise (or make up your own), and then return to it.

> *Note:* If possible, do this exercise sitting in a chair, not in bed, with the lights turned on.

Close your eyes, and breathe out three times slowly. See yourself in a meadow where the sun is high in the sky. Lie down, putting your head on a soft tuft of grass, and watch the sun set. See the sun descend slowly behind the horizon. When the sun has disappeared, and the sky is dark, see yourself leaving the meadow, and going to your bed and sleeping peacefully. Then breathe out one time slowly, open your eyes, turn off the lights, and go to bed.

Insomnia and Feeling Safe

A young man named Raul explained that he could fall asleep but not stay asleep. When he woke in the middle of the night, he would feel compelled to check all the windows and doors and then did a perimeter check of the home. After the check, he'd be alert and unable to fall asleep. I suggested he do an imaginal check before bed; if he awoke, he was to do the imaginal check first and then stop and ask himself if he still needed to carry out the physical check. By stopping a moment, he was giving himself a space of freedom to change his habit from hypervigilance to relaxed awareness and calm.

The Perimeter Check

Intention: To feel safe while you sleep.
Frequency: Each night before bed for 21 days. If desired, repeat for another two cycles of 21 days, stopping seven days between cycles. If you awaken during the night with an urge to do the physical check, do the imaginal exercise first, then ask yourself "Do I need to carry out the physical check?" If the answer is yes, by all means get up and do it.

Sit up (in bed or in a chair), close your eyes, and breathe out three times slowly. Imaginally check the perimeters of your house or apartment, including the yard, the garage, the balcony, roof, etc. Check all the corners on the floor and on the ceiling. As you check, place a blue eye of protection, a cross, or star of David, wherever is needed. Know that this eye (cross or star) shields you and your family from danger. Sense and feel it is safe to sleep through the night, knowing that you are safe. Breathe out once and go to bed.

Insomnia and Nightmares

Protection

Intention: To relax into a peaceful sleep that lasts the whole night through.
Frequency: Each night before going to sleep for 21 days or as needed.

Lying down with closed eyes, breathe out three times slowly. Draw a circle of (divine) love and protection around you and your family. In this circle, see and feel the white light of peace, the blue light of healing, the ruby-red light of joy, and the green light of safety and calm. No one and nothing may enter this circle if not for the greater good. Breathe out and go to sleep.

Emerald Dome

Intention: To sleep peacefully.
Frequency: Each night before going to sleep for 21 days or as needed.

Lying down, with eyes closed, breathe out three times slowly. See yourself enclosed within an emerald dome of peace. Sense and feel the glow of the verdant green light diffusing around you, permeating you, protecting you from any disturbing forces, inside or out. Feel your lungs, abdomen, and rib cage expanding and contracting with each breath. Feel your breath slowing down to a comfortable rhythm, natural and quiet. Feel your neck and jaw relaxing; feel your shoulders, arms, and fingers relaxing and becoming heavy; feel your hips and pelvis relaxing and becoming heavy; feel your legs, feet, and toes relaxing and becoming heavy, as you continue to breathe in the green calm and drift into sleep.

Ring of Fire

Intention: To feel protected at night.
Frequency: Each night before going to sleep for 21 days, or as needed.

Lying down, with eyes closed, breathe out three times slowly. Put an imaginal ring of fire around yourself, bed, or home, knowing that nothing and no one can harm you or your family and it is safe to sleep the whole night through. Breathe out and relax into sleep.

> *Note:* In the morning, when you awake, with eyes closed, imaginally remove the ring of fire, breathe out, and open your eyes.

Chinese Clay Warriors

Intention: To protect your home while you sleep.
Frequency: Each night before going to sleep for 21 days or as needed.

Sit up (in a chair or bed), close your eyes, and breathe out three times slowly. Imaginally check the perimeters of your house or apartment, including the yard, the garage, the balcony, roof, etc. Place giant, fierce clay warriors in a circle around your house or property. Breathe life into each of these warriors, one by one, as they take up their shields and weapons to protect you. Know that these great warriors fight to the death and will not let any intruders pass them. Sense and feel it is safe to sleep through the night, knowing that nothing can harm you or your family. Breathe out once, open your eyes, and go to bed.

Insomnia and Putting the Day Behind You

Sometimes your day intrudes into your night, preventing you from sleeping easily. **Reversing the Day** is a set of imagery exercises performed just before you go to bed. In them, you imaginally go over and review your day or part of your day *in reverse order*, correcting any difficulties — distressing feelings, conflictual interchanges with people, and events that went sour. The exercises clear your mind of the day's happenings so you can fall asleep easily. Practiced regularly, you can become aware of the habitual "negative" patterns and evolve new approaches, skills, and mechanisms for coping with daily difficulties. Below are three options for reversing the day, from easiest to the most complex.[5]

Option 1: **Reversing the Conflicts of the Day**

While you are lying in bed, with eyes closed, breathe out one time slowly and imaginally go over your day in REVERSE order, focusing on any conflictual situations. Start with the most recent disturbing event, then go back in time until you get to the first difficult event of the day. You can correct the events imaginally any way you wish.

For example, if you had an argument with someone:
- Just see yourself remaining calm, or walking away, or switching points of view so you adopt the other person's point of view and he or she adopts yours. Notice how you feel. In this way, you gain distance from your habitual responses and find new ways to respond to daily conflicts.
- Alternatively, you can take a golden pail of clear water and a golden brush and wipe away the "scene" or memory of the argument to the left, including the people and any disturbing feelings this evoked in you.

Option 2: Reversing a Trait

Choose a specific trait, habit, or feeling you wish to change. Any trait can be used — for example, fear, anger, grief, lassitude or inertia, addictive cravings, etc. For 21 nights, while you are lying in bed, with your eyes closed, breathe out one time slowly, and in your mind's eye review your day in REVERSE order imaginally, correcting any incident in which you experienced the trait, habit, or feeling.

Let's say you are abstaining from drinking alcohol. In reverse order, recall each time the craving came up during the day, and see yourself correcting the image any way you wish. For example, imaginally see yourself calling an AA buddy for support; taking the craving and redirecting it by taking an imaginal bike ride; imaginally excusing yourself from the social situation that is

Insomnia and Nightmares

stimulating the craving for the addicting substance; or just simply pushing the substance away in your mind's eye to the left, far away from you. *As you continue to do this for 21 days, you will slowly create a wedge between yourself and the trait. This wedge will help you become more aware of the triggers that stimulate the addictive craving or behavior.*

Below is the ultimate reversal exercise for self-transformation. It has a crossover effect for insomnia as well.

Option 3: **Living Your Day in Reverse**

While you are lying in bed, with your eyes closed, breathe out one time slowly and see yourself go over your day in REVERSE order, event by event. Start with the last event of the day and relive it in imagery, correcting your behavior as needed. Go to the next-to-last event and relive it, changing whatever needed correcting. Continue in reverse order until you reach the time when you woke up. Recall each event, obtain something for yourself you were not able to obtain during the day, and imaginally correct your attitude and behavior in those situations where you had difficulty.

To correct your attitude or behavior in a conflictual situation with another person, you can "reverse" your actual dialogue. For example, if you had a troubling conversation with someone, recall the conversation as close to verbatim as possible. Then imagine the other person's words coming out in your voice and your words coming out in his or her voice. As you do this you come to understand the other person's experience beyond your fixed ideas and judgments of what they are communicating to you. The next day, if you wish, you may call that person to patch things up or make amends. *You might find that you fall asleep without completing the entire exercise — that's fine.* It is the consistency of the practice that bears fruit.

> *Note:* You can complete any of these three reversing exercises by creating a new vision of tomorrow. With your eyes closed, see, sense, and feel yourself awakening to a new day, your entire being radiant with energy and good cheer.

Nightmares

Serena was a veteran of the first Gulf War who told me that every night when she went to bed and fell asleep, she relived the journey her battalion made north through the oil fields. In her dream, all the wells are on fire and dark black smoke fills the air, penetrating every inch of her lungs. Serena cannot take in a breath. It reminds her of the way she felt as a child when she suffered from asthma attacks that made her feel as if she were dying. She awoke each morning with a dry mouth, feeling exhausted. Her husband, John, added that while she was sleeping, she flailed her arms and legs and called out, but he couldn't understand what she was saying.

We worked together imaginally to reduce her nightmares. In her imagery work, with me as her guide, she went back into her dream to the point where she could not breathe easily. She imaginally put on a golden helmet and breathing apparatus suit so

Insomnia and Nightmares

she could breathe easily and freely.

When we close our eyes and go to sleep and dream, we step into a living movie of our lives. It is as if we are peering into a mirror and seeing ourselves reflected back to us. Similarly, in doing imaginal work, we also see ourselves reflected back in pictures. Dreams give us all sorts of useful information, including our wishes, our fears, our conflicts, and our relationship to others, as well as our health, new possibilities, and solutions to problems.

PTSD symptoms are reflected in dreams that often take the form of nightmares. These nightmares give us information about ourselves, as well as about what we still need to attend to. They are internal themes that we have not yet mastered. When we correct, reverse, and transform a nightmare, we become the one in charge, no longer a victim, but master of the event and master of the memory. We give ourselves a new direction that until now has been impeded. We reverse and rework the experience, reshaping our inner experience of reality, our outer-shared reality, and our ability to sleep peacefully.

On the next few pages are several imaginal exercises to effectively and safely deal with nightmares. Read through the following exercises and choose the ones that resonate within you.

IMAGERY EXERCISES FOR NIGHTMARES

Strong Box

Intention: To dispose of your nightmares.
Frequency: Before bed for 21 days. If desired, repeat for another two cycles of 21 days, stopping seven days between cycles.

Sit up in bed, close your eyes, and breathe out three times slowly. Take your nightmare and put it inside a box with a heavy, strong lid. Then, seal the box closed. Put the sealed box into an impermeable, lead-lined vault and seal the vault. Bury it deep in the earth or at the bottom of the ocean.

Breathe out one time slowly and deeply. Notice your body relaxing all over, letting go of any tension you may be feeling. Sense and know that you are safe and nothing can harm you. With eyes closed, lie down and let yourself drift into sleep.

Conquering the Dragon of Fear

Intention: To sleep peacefully.
Frequency: Before bed for 21 days.

Sit up in bed, close your eyes, and breathe out three times slowly. See the dragon of fear. Have with you whatever you need to protect yourself and defeat this beast. Conquer the dragon in any way you please, sensing and feeling that you are becoming your own hero and there is nothing to fear.

Insomnia and Nightmares

Breathe out one time slowly and deeply. Notice your body relaxing all over, letting go of any tension you may be feeling. Sense and know that you and your loved ones are safe and nothing can harm you. With eyes closed, lie down and let yourself drift into sleep.

> *Note*: Do this next exercise **only** after you have been practicing the imagery in this book for some time. Read through this entire exercise before trying it. If you feel anxious, skip it.

The Movie Channel

Intention: To rid yourself of nightmares.

Frequency: Do every morning for 21 days. If you are no longer having the nightmares, stop doing the exercise. If the nightmares persist, continue to do the exercise for another two cycles of 21 days, stopping for seven days between cycles.

Close your eyes and breathe out slowly three times. See yourself in front of your TV screen. Push the remote control until you get to the setting called "happy memories" channel. View several happy memories from your life. Breathe out one time. Now use the remote control to go to the "repeating nightmare" channel. There on the screen in front of you, see the single *most* significant image of one of your nightmares. Breathe out one time slowly. What is the feeling or sensation associated with viewing this image on the screen? Now edit this disturbing image by pushing it out of the screen to the left and replace with a new positive image — one where you are in control and can rewrite the script to include an ending that works for you. With that new, corrected image, what feeling emerges? Breathe out one time and open your eyes.

> *Note:* If you wake up in the middle of the night with the nightmare, breathe out three times slowly and recall the corrected image for a few seconds.

PHYSICAL EXERCISE FOR PROTECTION

Put an amulet — an object that protects you from harm — above your bed or under your pillow. It can be a rosary, cross, dream-catcher, Egyptian ankh, David's star, hamsa (protective hand), blue protective eye, or any other good luck charm that makes you know that you are warding off evil, bad dreams, and fear.

> *Note:* Do **NOT** use a physical weapon such as a gun or knife under your pillow for protection.

CHAPTER 12

Loss and Grief

Grief is found in every culture. Even animals mourn their dead and apparently feel distress while doing so. There is no right or wrong way to mourn. Various people in various cultures mourn in a multitude of ways, and it is important that you find a way that is either part of your family or religious tradition or that in another way feels right for you.

Sometimes circumstances (being caught up in a war or part of an illness epidemic, for example) make it impossible to stop and take the time to mourn. But most people need to mourn before they can get back to their usual routines. Delayed mourning usually means that at some time the need to mourn will arise, be it a month later or 30 years later.

Most often, when a person goes into a state of mourning, they feel the need for community support. Most religions, including Christianity, Judaism, Hinduism, Buddhism, and Islam, have prescribed ways of mourning. Some have prescribed ways of ending the mourning period, too, such as the ceremony for placing the gravestone on the grave after 11 months — a ceremony in Judaism called unveiling.

Even when there is no religious form of mourning within a given culture, there are other tried-and-true methods that help people get through the mourning process. Going to a church and lighting a candle for one's loved one, visiting with relatives of the deceased, donating something in the deceased's honor, creating a scholarship fund or a work of art in memory of the loved one — all these help a person come to a sense of peace that the deceased will not be forgotten and that their name will live on.

Everett came to my office one December morning in such distress that he was hardly able to speak. He had just found out that his best friend in the Marines, who had been given orders to remain in Afghanistan while the rest of the unit was shipped back to the States, had been killed the day before by a roadside bomb. Everett was devastated that he hadn't even been able to say goodbye, since his buddy had left the area before the others shipped out. He couldn't bear the thought that his friend had died alone, without anyone he knew beside him to comfort him as the medics tried unsuccessfully to save his life.

"I don't have time to mourn Dan," Everett said. " I have to finish reports before we ship out again in two weeks, and I need to spend time with my family."

"How did it go for you today at work? I asked.

"Really bad. Awful." Everett said. "I couldn't get anything done."

"And why do you think that is?" I asked. I knew Everett knew the answer.

"I am so sad," he answered. "And angry. I should have been there."

I worked with Everett to release the grief and guilt, at first

Loss and Grief

through acknowledging the pain and then through the imagery exercises below.

❖

A Vietnam veteran I had been seeing for about a year arrived one Tuesday morning with his wife, whom I had not met.

"We have a problem," Andy said, "and we have been fighting about it and we need you to help us solve it." While Andy had been on his last tour of duty several years before, his wife, Anna, had given birth to a baby girl who had suddenly died the next day. Anna had had the infant cremated and put the ashes in an urn on the mantle, and there it had remained for all these years. They had gone on to have two more children, a girl and a boy; their firstborn, the child who had died, had never been given a name.

Now they were expecting their first grandchild and were talking about the christening. Anna felt they had to do something about their own child, but Andy didn't agree. He wanted to "leave well enough alone."

"It was all a long time ago," said Andy.

"Yes, but I am still grieving, and I need closure," said Anna.

After some discussion, where each expressed their needs and their feelings about the deceased baby, they both agreed that they should do something as a family to mark the birth and death of their first child, and finally bury her and give her a name to be inscribed on a tombstone. So they bought a plot at the cemetery, asked their minister to officiate, and invited their two living adult children and their spouses to attend the burial of their sister, whom they had decided to name Ashley.

The next week, Andy reported to me that he and Anna had never been closer, that they felt they had done the right thing. Their kids had both said they appreciated having a service for their deceased sister where the family could all grieve together.

The act of grieving is a process, best explained by Dr. Elisabeth Kübler-Ross in her book *On Death and Dying*.[6] Her belief was that the grieving process occurs over time in five stages: denial, anger, bargaining, depression, and acceptance. Knowing about and seeing ourselves in relationship to these varying and sometimes overlapping stages can help us cope with our loss.

IMAGERY EXERCISES FOR LOSS AND GRIEF

Laying the Dead to Rest

Intention: To lay the dead to rest; to complete grieving.
Frequency: Do one time in the morning for seven days.

Close your eyes and breathe out three times slowly. See yourself entering the cemetery through a gate. At the gravesite, see the friends and family of the deceased gathered together. See yourself recovering the body of your dead comrade. See the body of your friend or comrade now laid out peacefully. Recite a prayer or meditation over the body as you rebury it. Put flowers on the grave. Leave the cemetery by the way you came in, reciting the prayer or meditation as you walk away, going out of the gate, closing the gate behind you. Breathe out and open your eyes.

> *Note*: If there is more than one deceased, rebury each one individually, reciting a prayer for each person.

Clearing the Tears

Intention: Releasing sorrow.
Frequency: Twice a day, in the morning and before bed, for 21 days.

Close your eyes and breathe out three times slowly. Imagine a lake in the sky. See that it is a lake of tears. Breathe out. A drop of water falls from a cloud above onto the lake of tears; this added drop is a tipping point, stirring up pain within you. Breathe out. See, sense, and feel this lake of tears evaporating, dried by the sun, rising to form a white cloud above that dissipates into the bright blue sky. Breathe out and open your eyes.

Bouncing Into Graceland

Intention: To heal grief and guilt.
Frequency: Twice a day, in the morning upon rising and before bed.

Close your eyes and breathe out slowly three times. See yourself as a pilgrim traveling on the road to Graceland. Sense that your traveling companions are not only living family members but ghosts of companions long gone. Know that soldiers, sinners, and saints are also received in Graceland. Breathe out one time. See, sense, and feel how losing loved ones is like a strong wind blowing the window of your heart open. Breathe out one time.

Feel yourself as a human trampoline — falling, flying, or tumbling into Graceland. Breathe out one time. Feel and know that you have reached a place of no obligations and duties. Accept and understand that each person has a unique destiny to fulfill — and you cannot walk the path of another. Know that the dead come to heal the living. Hear the message that a dead companion who was close to you has to tell you. Breathe out one time. Sense and feel your broken heart mended by these dead loved ones. Breathe out one time. Having been received in Graceland, you are freed from the past in order to create your own life anew. See, sense, and feel yourself walking upright to a new future. What do you discover? Breathe out and open your eyes.

PHYSICAL EXERCISES FOR BEREAVEMENT

Activities to help jolt you out of the depths of bereavement:
1. Request a mass for a Catholic loved one — light a candle for them while you are there.
2. Visit the parents, other relatives, or significant others of the deceased.

Loss and Grief

3. Name a bench for or plant a tree in honor of the person you loved.
4. Donate something meaningful in memory of your lost friend — a book to a library, a basketball to a boys and girls club, etc.
5. Visit the gravesite — if the deceased was cremated, find a place where you spent time together and go there — and tell the loved one how much you miss them and the ways in which you are including their memory in your life.

CHAPTER 13

Physical Pain

Due to the many extreme physical tasks soldiers, sailors, and Marines are asked to do on a daily basis, not to mention the consequences of physical injury, many combatants and veterans deal with a substantial amount of physical pain. Pain comes from many quarters, including injury from combat and from duty, such as hurting one's back by carrying a 100-pound backpack or falling when the ship lists during a storm.

All too often, physical pain is a trigger for a feeling or emotion that reminds us of the trauma. Dealing with chronic pain is an invitation for us to observe and learn how physical pain translates into feelings of anger, depression, or anxiety. Understanding the body–mind connection and how each influences the other is a first step to reducing chronic pain.

The best way to start reversing the pain and begin healing is to break the pain cycle. In addition to mental imagery, medication can be effective, as can body work such as physical therapy, massage, Feldenkrais, acupuncture, and the like. Awareness of how we hold the body, how we sleep, how we chronically tense our muscles and create spasms are all important to learn about and master.

Physical Pain

❖

Jeremy was a 29-year-old veteran of the war in Afghanistan when I met him. He had lost a leg when an IED exploded, and even though three years had passed, he still had some phantom pain, especially at night when he was trying to go to sleep. Pain was easier for him to manage during the daytime, because he was training at least four hours a day for the triathlon in the Paralympics. He was married and the father of a young son whom he adored, and he and his wife, Emily, had gotten through the difficult first year after his injury and were doing well. He was taking a narcotic both for the pain and to help him sleep, but sometimes he would still wake at night in tremendous pain.

Jeremy said he wanted to find a natural way to overcome the pain, since if he took too much medicine, especially during the day, he felt drowsy and overmedicated and could not properly train. So together we made a list of images that would help him counteract the pain imaginally. The images he came up with were: opening the jaws of a lion, huge waves rolling over him on the beach and taking the pain away with it, and lying for short periods on a bed made of ice. Over intervals of three weeks, Jeremy practiced each of these exercises in the morning and at sundown; at the end of nine weeks, he reported that his pain was between 70 and 90 percent better, which was enough to allow him to get back to sleep whenever he awakened in pain.

IMAGERY EXERCISES FOR PAIN

The Question Mark

Intention: To heal back issues, to remove doubt, to overcome difficulties around money or relationships.
Frequency: Morning, evening, and before bed for 21 days, and whenever you feel back pain, fatigue, or defeated.

Close your eyes and breathe out three times slowly. See yourself, in profile, in the shape of a question mark. Notice the expression on your face. Breathe out one time. Now see yourself in profile becoming an exclamation point as you face forward. How do you look and feel? Breathe out and open your eyes.

Hurling into Space

Intention: To get rid of head pain.
Frequency: Use as needed.

Close your eyes and breathe out three times slowly. See yourself putting the points of pain on a spaceship that shoots out of your head and disappears into deep space. Breathe out and open your eyes.

Through the Magnifying Glass

Intention: To diminish pain.
Frequency: Use as needed.

Close your eyes and breathe out once. See your pain and look at it from every angle through a magnifying glass. Erase it by wiping it away to the left. Breathe out and open your eyes.

Painless Voyage

Intention: To dissolve pain.
Frequency: Use as needed.

Close your eyes and breathe out three times slowly. See the pain. Shrink yourself down very small and enter your body through the pores of your skin or any orifice. Holding a golden can of oil, make your way to the pain. Have a light with you and examine the pain from every angle. Then pour the hot, golden oil over the pain, covering it completely. See the pain dissolve into a golden point. Turn around and see golden rays of health and well-being flowing from this point to all parts of your body. Know that the warm, bright oil is curing the area and reducing the pain. Then leave your body by the route by which you entered, sensing your pain has gone. Breathe out and open your eyes.

The Crystal Light

Intention: To take away pain.
Frequency: Use as needed.

Close your eyes and breathe out three times slowly. Imagine yourself holding a pure, unblemished crystal between the forefingers of your right and left hands. Take the crystal and place it over the area of pain. See a beam of strong green light coming from above, streaming through the crystal. As it streams through, the light diffuses into the pain and absorbs the pain. Know that the pain is being consumed by the green light. Sense and feel what has happened and notice how you look. Breathe out and open your eyes.

Heavy Hands

Intention: To remove pain.
Frequency: Use as needed.

Close your eyes and breathe out three times slowly. Imagine your arms and hands becoming very, very heavy. Notice that there is a giant stone sitting on top of your hands, making them numb. Then place your numb hands over the area of pain, knowing that they are absorbing all the pain from that spot. Sense what happens; notice how you look, and know that the pain is gone. Breathe out and open your eyes.

The Octopus

Intention: To heal joint and muscle pain and dissolve arthritic nodules.
Frequency: Use as needed.

Close your eyes and breathe out three times slowly. See your arms (or legs, or fingers, or toes) as octopus tentacles, sinewy and undulating, elongating out in front of you for at least a mile. See and sense the flexibility of these arms elongating freely, allowing you to bend them in all directions. Breathe out and open your eyes, knowing that the pain is gone and movement is restored.

Green Leaf

Intention: For pain and general healing.
Frequency: Morning, evening, and before bed for 21 days.

Close your eyes, breathing out three times slowly. Imagine yourself in the backyard of a house. It is autumn and the leaves are falling from the trees. They are yellow, orange, and red. With a rake in hand, begin raking the leaves toward the back end of the garden. Make a pile with the leaves and then burn them. Take a small shovel and dig a hole nearby. Take the ashes and bury them and with them your past difficulties. Cover over the hole.

Breathe out. Walking back toward the house, a leaf falls from the tree, touches you on the head, and falls to the ground. Pick up this autumn leaf and hold it in your left hand. Cover that hand with your right hand. Feel a pulsation there. Uncover your left hand, and see the leaf turning partly green. Cover your left hand again. Feel the pulsation getting stronger. Uncover your hand again. See the leaf now three-quarters green. Cover your hand once more. Feel the pulsation getting stronger still. Remove your hand. See the leaf fully green and alive.

Breathe out. Place the leaf over any part of your body that needs care or healing. Sense and feel the sap from the leaf entering the affected area, knowing that the healing is taking place. See the area healed up, looking like the healthy tissue around it. Silently, say the word *healing* to yourself. Notice the feeling and any sensation that may accompany it. Breathe out and open your eyes.

Green Meadow

Intention: To heal pain.
Frequency: Morning, evening, and before bed for 21 days.

Close your eyes and breathe out three times slowly. Imagine you are in a very green meadow on the bank of a small stream that flows fast from a high hill. See yourself picking flowers in this green meadow. Lie in the grass and put the flowers you picked on the parts of your body that are giving you difficulty. Breathe out. Sense the sap of the flowers entering your body, rejuvenating and refreshing you with their richness and life force. Remove the flowers from your body when they start to wilt. Stand up and

Physical Pain

throw them into a stream that flows into a creek, then a river, and out to sea. Know that these currents of water are taking away the problems of the past so they do not return. Breathe out and open your eyes.

Falling Out of Adversity

Intention: To rise above physical and mental pain.
Frequency: Twice a day, morning and before bed, for 21 days.

Close your eyes and breathe out three times slowly. Looking into a mirror, see yourself:
- Falling into adversity...
  Breathe out one time.
- Falling into heavy depression...
  Breathe out one time.
- Falling into apathy...
  Breathe out one time.
- Becoming light and full of gladness...

Breathe out one time slowly, and see yourself naked in the mirror. See, sense, and feel yourself healthy — being made healthy by the mind and being made happy by the mind even though there are (or may be) physical infirmities. Breathe out and open your eyes.

Heartache

Intention: To remove pain, anger, and fear; to detoxify the body.
Frequency: Once a day in the morning upon awakening for 21 days.

Close your eyes and breathe out three times slowly. See the pain in your heart as a dark reddish color. Remove your heart gently from your chest. Take it in your hands. Sense your heart beating irregularly from fear and anxiety. Throw it, with tremendous force, to the far reaches of the galaxy until it reaches Sirius, the Dog Star.

Breathe out. See a winged heart returning into your body having recovered health, intelligence, and love. See, sense, and feel a blue light streaming out of the heart and flowing into the blood vessels of the body. The blue light forms halos around all the red blood cells, enriching them, making them strong, healthy, and alive. Sense the blood flowing evenly and rhythmically throughout the body. See and sense the blood flow through the kidneys, thoroughly cleansing you of fear and toxins. See the blood flow into the liver, thoroughly cleansing you of anger and toxins. See the liver regenerating itself, growing new healthy cells encased in a cocoon of blue light. Breathe out and open your eyes.

The Magnet of Health

Intention: To remove shrapnel that is causing you pain.
Frequency: Morning, evening, and before bed for 21 days.

Close your eyes and breathe out three times slowly. Imagine you are holding a strong magnet. Place it near the area of your body that has the shrapnel lodged in it that is causing you pain. Move the magnet up and down the area three times, seeing and sensing the shrapnel particles being pulled out of you through your pores. Hear the clink of the particles as they adhere to the magnet. Now, apply a blue-golden salve mixed of sun and sky to heal the damaged soft tissue and bone. See all the cells filling in the tissue and bone where the shrapnel was removed. Then take the magnet and shrapnel particles and toss them into a recycling bin. Breathe out and open your eyes.

> *Note:* If the shrapnel is not causing pain or other problems, no need to do this exercise. For pins/screws/metal plates/rods, imaginally shave down the plate or rod in the painful areas to relieve the pressure on the surrounding tissue, and then imaginally remove the shaved-down shards.

Sandpaper

Intention: To rid yourself of pain.
Frequency: Morning, evening, and before bed for 21 days.

Close your eyes and breathe out three times slowly. See and sense your pain as a black blob. Have with you a piece of golden sandpaper. Sand away the sharp edges, or spikes, or nails, knowing that as you are sanding down the edges, they are losing their force and influence, and the blob is disappearing.

Take whatever remains of the blob and hurl it into the stratosphere, knowing that your pain is gone. Breathe out and open your eyes.

Creating Your Own Natural "Pain-killer" Exercise

Intention: To rid yourself of pain.
Frequency: As needed, or do it rhythmically, three times daily, for 21 days.

Remember, every word has a corresponding image!

Close your eyes, breathe out three times, and ask yourself: *What does this pain look like?* See, sense, and feel the pain. Now get rid of it. Remember, this is the imagination, and *anything is possible*. Have with you whatever or whomever you need. (For example: a golden lasso, a golden pick or hammer, a light, a vacuum

Physical Pain

cleaner, blue ice, Mr. Freeze, little Pac-Men that can gobble up pain, a healing salve, the Archangel Raphael, a lock and key, a million endorphin molecules, etc.) Once you have gotten rid of, transformed, or changed the pain, breathe out and open your eyes.

The Milky Way of Health

Intention: To restore health and vitality.
Frequency: Morning, evening, and before bed for 21 days.

Close your eyes and breathe out three times slowly. Take your limb or body part (or phantom limb) that is hurting and *quickly* hurl it into the Milky Way, far, far away.

Breathe out. Now, see a new limb or body part, perfectly formed and free of defect, being tossed back to you from deep space. Retrieve this body part, and sense and feel it merging and melding with the rest of you, bringing new life and vitality to the area. Breathe out and open your eyes.

IMAGERY EXERCISE FOR PHANTOM LIMB PAIN

An innovative, successful new medical treatment for phantom limb pain uses a specially constructed *physical* mirror to retrain the brain and nervous system.[7] Using this therapy, a person looks into this unique mirror and sees only the reflection of their uninjured limbs (i.e., the uninjured limb is reflected back on both the right and left side of the body). This allows the person to see themselves in the mirror as whole — having two complete arms and two complete legs. In this therapy, the person physically moves the uninjured limb and simultaneously sees both of his limbs as moving whole and complete in the mirror.

The reflection in the mirror of a completely normal body tricks the brain and nervous system into having to reorganize and integrate the mismatch between proprioception[8] and visual feedback from the trick mirror, thus healing the pain and sense of loss. In other words, if the brain believes and experiences that the limb is intact, it stops sending out phantom pain signals.

Here is an imaginal mirror exercise to reduce phantom limb pain by implanting a new somatic memory into your brain and nervous system. Just as you can change the "emotional" memory of an event, so can change the "somatic" (i.e., bodily) memory of the event of the injured or lost limb. Remember, anything is possible in the imagination.

Seeing Yourself Whole

Intention: To reduce pain and discomfort of the phantom limb; to change the somatic memory of the amputated/phantom limb from missing and painful to whole, complete, and comfortable.

Frequency: Four times a day, morning, noon, evening, and before bed, for 21 days. Repeat for two cycles of 21 days, stopping for seven days between cycles.

Physical Pain

Close your eyes and breathe out three times, counting backward from three to one, each outbreath being a new number. At one, see yourself becoming strong and tall, then breathe out again, and see the one becoming a zero and the zero growing in size and becoming a large mirror. Look into the mirror and see yourself whole and complete, with all four limbs intact and whole — the phantom leg or arm is now perfectly formed and functional. See, sense, and feel that this limb is a perfect copy, a mirror image, of the other, uninjured limb. Breathe out one time. Now see, sense, and feel the two limbs (either both arms or both legs) moving together — as the healthy arm or leg moves, so does its opposite. See, sense, and feel both sides stretching out, bending and rotating at their joints normally.

For example:

- If, in waking life, the phantom arm or leg feels cramped, see, sense, and feel both arms (or legs) uncurling, stretched out and relaxed.
- If, in waking life, the phantom arm (or leg) feels rotated or out of place, see, sense, and feel both sides, right and left, rotating fully around the shoulder or hip joint, moving freely in all directions, sensing both sides are perfectly placed in the joint.
- If, when you walk, there is tingling, numbness, or pain, now see, sense, and feel both sides relaxed, normal, at ease, and comfortable.

Now, see yourself dancing, knowing that your arms and legs are all reunited, acting, working, and mirroring each other in perfect harmony. When all is in place, breathe out, counting forward from one to three, each outbreath being a new number. Then open your eyes and, for a moment, see on the wall in front of you an image of yourself whole and complete.

CHAPTER 14

Concussions and Mild Traumatic Brain Injury

Concussions or mild traumatic brain injury (mTBI) can create physical, mental, emotional, and behavioral difficulties. Many veterans of combat complain of a wide variety of symptoms, including: fatigue, difficulty sleeping, headaches, visual disturbances, dizziness/balance problems, poor attention and difficulty concentrating, memory loss, getting lost or confused, slowness in thinking, difficulty making decisions, mood changes, nausea, loss of smell, anger, frustration, impulsivity, depression, and anxiety.

Scattered throughout this volume are imagery exercises that address shared PTSD and mTBI issues. Below are specific imagery exercises to heal the brain and nervous system.

❖

Amos, a veteran of the first Gulf War, had been aboard ship in rough seas when a shelf full of supplies came loose and fell on him, knocking him to the ground. As he fell, he hit his head hard on the edge of a metal door and was knocked unconscious. He reported that after that incident, he never felt like himself again. He struggled to remember things, had frequent headaches, sometimes felt dizzy, and had ringing in his ears. When on duty, he sometimes had a delayed response to questions he was asked. He also found he was irritable, had mood swings, had trouble sleeping, and could no longer taste the flavors of the food he ate.

It took many years until enough research had been done on traumatic brain injury and Amos was able to get the help he needed. His assessment at the VA showed that he had mild TBI, and he began treatment at the TBI clinic. He received several kinds of therapy, including physical, occupational, and vestibular therapy to help with balance and ringing in the ears. Along with these physical interventions, he began using a smartphone to help him keep track of things he needed to remember, and he went to his "mental gym" each day and practiced some of the exercises below. He reported that all of the efforts he made paid off, and that he felt better and better as time went on.

IMAGERY EXERCISES FOR CONCUSSIONS AND MILD TRAUMATIC BRIAN INJURY

Orange Tree

Intention: To heal brain injury, to create internal order.
Frequency: Morning, evening, and before bed for 21 days.

Concussions and Mild Traumatic Brain Injury

Close your eyes and breathe out three times slowly. Find yourself in a garden. There is a beautiful orange tree with no fruit. The crown of the tree is uneven. Climb a ladder, with garden clippers in hand, and trim and prune the branches so that the crown of the tree is evenly shaped. Make sure that none of the branches are intertwined, and remove all that are weak or not in place. Descend the ladder, smell the fragrant orange blossoms, and see the oranges ripening. Know that your brain is healing. Breathe out and open your eyes.

The Matrix of Healing

Intention: To heal brain injury.
Frequency: Morning, evening, and before bed for 21 days.

Close your eyes and breathe out three times slowly. Gently, take your brain and place it into your small intestine.[9] See, sense, and feel your brain being restored to its original wholeness. Place it gently back into your head, knowing that you are coming into order. Breathe out and open your eyes.

Aladdin's Turban

Intention: To feel balanced and clearheaded.
Frequency: Once in the morning upon awakening and as often as needed during the day for 21 days.

Close your eyes and breathe out three times slowly. Imagine that you are wearing a white silk turban. As you put it on in front of a mirror, you feel balanced, centered, and focused, knowing that your head and brain are coming into order. Breathe out and open your eyes.

Vase of Blue Light

Intention: To heal the brain.
Frequency: Morning, evening, and before bed for 21 days.

Close your eyes and breathe out three times slowly. See yourself as a blue vase absorbing blue light through all your pores. See, sense, and feel this blue light filling you completely from head to toe. This light fills your brain and skull, removing inflammation and repairing any neural damage. See how, as a crystal vessel full of blue light, you have a clarity reflecting the blue of the ocean, the blue of Heaven. Breathe out and open your eyes.

The Flashlight

Intention: To heal concussion of the brain.
Frequency: Morning, evening, and before bed for 21 days.

Close your eyes and breathe out three times slowly. Gently take the top of your skull off and put it on a sky blue velvet pillow near you. Have a golden flashlight in hand and turn it on. It beams a white healing light. Shine the light into your brain to discover the areas that need special healing and let the light linger there. See, sense, and feel the white light healing the brain tissue until it is healthy and bright. Turn off the flashlight so you can use it again; then put the top of your skull back in its proper place, knowing that you are healing. Breathe out and open your eyes.

Shampooing the Brain

Intention: To heal from traumatic brain injuries.
Frequency: Morning, evening, and before bed for 21 days.

Close your eyes and breathe out three times slowly. Wash your hair with shampoo and sparkling water. If any section of your hair is not bright, see how the light from above makes it shine. Delicately cut around the circumference of your head. Remove the top of your cranium carefully as you would remove the top of a round box. Using your hair, gently sweep out your brain, cleaning out all the debris, bruises, wounds, and any disturbance. Sense and feel that you are becoming more alert and focused. When all is clean, put the top of your head back gently and glue it carefully with a blue-golden gel. Then wash your hair once again. Breathe out and open your eyes.

The Lake of the Brain

Intention: To regulate intracranial brain pressure and headaches.
Frequency: Morning, evening, and before bed for 21 days.

Close your eyes and breathe out three times slowly. Look down at the top of your head. Lift off the top of your skull as if you were removing the top of the shell of a soft-boiled egg. Look inside. See the fluid of your brain and the moving nerve fibers that look like water plants beneath the surface. See the fluid draining out of your head. Sense and feel the tension relieved throughout your skull, the base of your skull, and the back of your neck as the fluid moves down the spinal column to its base at the tailbone. See fresh fluid moving up the spinal column, drawing the healing energies of the earth up through the neck and filling your skull with clean, clear liquid that bathes the nerve fibers that are floating within the fluid. Feel and sense the flow of fresh blood through your neck and down into the rest of your body. Put on the top of your skull, breathe out and open your eyes.

The Room of Silence
(To reduce tinnitus)
- See page 41 -

Bells and Chimes
(For single-eared tinnitus)

Intention: To heal tinnitus and restore hearing.
Frequency: Four times a day, morning, noon, evening, and before bed for 21 days.

Close your eyes and breathe out three times slowly. Imagine your undamaged ear growing larger. Hear a beautiful melody, church bells, or wind chimes sounding in the undamaged ear. Hear the healing sounds neutralizing the noise of the tinnitus in the impaired ear. Breathe out and open your eyes.

Valley of Peace

Intention: To heal tinnitus and alleviate anxiety.
Frequency: Morning, noon, evening, and before bed for 21 days.

Close your eyes and breathe out three times slowly. Imagine you are descending into a valley surrounded by a high, golden, soundproof wall. Lying down on a tuft of grass, see the setting sun in the distance and hear the birds chirping, announcing the close of day. Sense the peace descending on the valley as evening falls. Breathe out and open your eyes.

> *Note:* Vietnam vets should NOT do the following exercise.

Through the Jungle

Intention: To clear away confusion.
Frequency: Morning, evening, and before bed for 21 days.

Close your eyes and breathe out three times slowly. See yourself in the jungle of inner confusion or turmoil. The vines are entangling you. You are carrying a golden machete and are dressed in protective jungle gear.

Breathe out one time and cut your way through the tangle of vines, clearing a path in front of you. Know as you do so that you are disentangling yourself from confusion. Breathe out one time. In front of you is a golden bridge to a new future. Cross the bridge and see a golden path ahead of you. Take the path and discover what is there for you. Breathe out and open your eyes.

CHAPTER 15

Overcoming Addiction

It is not uncommon for combat veterans and active-duty personnel to turn to drugs and alcohol to try to cope with symptoms of PTSD and pain. You may have trouble falling asleep and then once asleep, have nightmares that awaken you, making it harder to fall asleep again. You might start by having a beer or a joint before bedtime, but soon you need more alcohol or drugs to feel relaxed. This coping behavior escalates until you may be drinking a six-pack or smoking several joints a day to calm down enough to fall asleep. While initially alcohol may make you sleepy, ultimately it disturbs the sleep cycle, so you never enter the stage of restful, restorative sleep. Before long, you may find yourself addicted to your substance of choice. At this point, you may have symptoms of both PTSD and a substance abuse problem. And since alcohol is a depressant, it can exacerbate depression.

❖

Michael is a Vietnam veteran who saw heavy combat. His best friend was killed in an ambush in the jungle, and Michael himself lost a foot when he stepped on a booby trap while on patrol. When he got back from the war, he remembers a group of protesters meeting his plane at the airport and calling him and his buddies "baby killers." When he got back home to Denver, he dared not mention that he was a veteran; nobody wanted to hear it. He became more and more depressed and found he could not fall asleep at night. He started drinking beer just before bed. When his worried father protested that his was son was becoming an alcoholic, Michael switched to marijuana. Soon he couldn't get through the day without smoking or fall asleep without being stoned. He dropped out of school because he couldn't concentrate. He then lost a series of jobs because he couldn't get up early enough to make it to work on time. His parents finally kicked him out, and Michael ended up homeless for two years, until finally a veterans' group found him under a highway overpass and got him into rehab. He went to the VA medical center and was given medicine to help him sleep and a better-fitting prosthesis so he was not in pain all the time. He started attending an AA group for combat veterans and has now been clean and sober for 17 years. He says the biggest help was turning his troubles over to a higher power and learning to love experiencing the world directly, instead of through the hazy filter of drugs. While the drugs blocked the pain, they also prevented him from experiencing the joys of life. Together we worked on deeper issues underlying the urge to drink by using the **Ra** and **Inner Journey** exercises that follow.

Overcoming Addiction

> *Note:* In addition to the imagery exercises that follow, see Chapter 17 for Stopping Exercises and Life Plan to curb addictions.

IMAGERY EXERCISES FOR OVERCOMING ADDICTION

Golden Ladder

Intention: To rid yourself of an addictive substance.
Frequency: Morning, evening, and before bed for 21 days. If desired, repeat for an additional two cycles of 21 days, stopping seven days between cycles.

   Close your eyes and breathe out three times slowly. Imagine a golden ladder standing erect in the middle of a field of fresh grass. It has 10 rungs. Starting at the bottom rung, notice what you are wearing and have the addictive substance (alcohol, drugs, cigarettes, etc.) in your hand.
   Breathe out one time. Begin to climb slowly until you reach the third rung. Look around, up and down, to survey the environment and notice how you are dressed. Then look at the substance to see what it looks like, and note how you feel.
   Breathe out one time and climb slowly to the fifth rung. Look around, up and down, and notice how you are dressed. Then look

at the substance and note how you feel.

Breathe out one time and climb slowly to the eighth rung and repeat the process.

Breathe out one time and climb slowly to the ninth rung and repeat the process again.

Breathe out one time and climb slowly to the 10th rung. At the 10th rung, note what the substance looks like. Take what you are now holding and throw it BEHIND you. Do not look at it. Notice how you look and feel. Then slide down the ladder *quickly*. At the base, again see how you look, feel, and are dressed. Know that you are freeing yourself from the addiction. Experience this new feeling. Come back to the chair, feel your feet planted firmly on the ground, breathe out, and open your eyes.

> *Note:* If the substance disappears before the 10th rung, you need not go farther up the ladder. Just start the descent down at the rung of freedom.

Serpent in the Sun

Intention: To rid yourself of an addictive substance.
Frequency: Morning, evening, and before bed for 21 days.

Close your eyes and breathe out three times slowly. See the serpent of addiction entering the sun and being burned up. See him vomiting the evil he has made. See the Egyptian sun god, Ra, kissing the poison and magically turning the serpent's vomit into gold.

Breathe out one time. Let this golden light fill you inside and out, above and below, knowing that your addiction is disappearing. Breathe out and open your eyes.

RA
- See page 75 -

Walking Straight, Walking Tall

Intention: To become sober.
Frequency: Morning, evening and before bed for 21 days.

Close your eyes and breathe out three times slowly. Imagine yourself, intoxicated or drunk, walking on a dark street, wobbling to and fro, seeing with double vision, out of balance.

Breathe out one time. Come into a brightly lit street full of sunshine. Feel its rays permeating and penetrating you. Sense and feel yourself suddenly becoming upright, walking straight and determined, sober, and with clear vision. See clearly where you are going and what is waiting for you on this new road. Remember what you have discovered. Breathe out and open your eyes.

Heartache
- See page 120 -

Inner Journey

Intention: Overcoming addiction.
Frequency: Once in the morning for seven or 21 days.

Close your eyes and breathe out three times slowly. Live and know how the little child within us is asking for immediate gratification.

Breathe out one time. Know that fulfilling immediate gratification is our desire to receive and not to give.

Breathe out one time. Live and know that our tendency for immediate gratification leads to restless searching.

Breathe out one time. Live and know that immediate gratification is asking for freedom but is pushing us to avoid commitments, involvements, and lifestyles that would bring such freedom.

Breathe out one time. Feel and know that when we go to extremes, we become self-absorbed and oriented and preoccupied only with ourselves.

Breathe out one time. Feel and know the difference between the true search for self and the self-indulgence that brings with it social alienation.

Breathe out one time. Feel and know the difference between self-indulgent introspection and engaging in a search for greater awareness and meaning.

Breathe out one time. See and know how working with images is a way of organizing reality and finding meaning.

Breathe out one time. Recognize that when you cut away from a habitual way of living that is familiar, you may feel empty.

Overcoming Addiction

Breathe out one time. Sense in yourself the clash between the two desires to both hold on to the habit and to let it go. Sense it as a war within yourself.

Breathe out one time. Recognize the way to repair and cure it. Feel and know how you often create problems in your life because you need their gifts.

Breathe out and open your eyes.

CHAPTER 16
Military Sexual Trauma

Few things are more difficult to deal with than sexual trauma in the military. While the experience of being raped or molested is horrible under any circumstance, being molested by a fellow service member, especially by someone senior in rank, is particularly violating — not only physically but to one's very creed of honor. Unlike other forms of trauma, it is a directed *personal* assault. When service members work together, the feeling is one of brotherhood and sisterhood, of a family, and when a person is raped by a fellow soldier, sailor, or Marine, the feeling can be similar to that of incest. Equally terrible, when people are sexually assaulted by persons of higher rank, the victims' helpless feelings of disbelief and the violation of trust can and often do turn to hopeless rage when they are threatened with losing their jobs or demotion in rank if they report the assault.

If victims report the assault, too often they find they are stonewalled in bringing the perpetrator to justice, since it means that the commanding officer must fill out piles of paperwork. Furthermore, the perception from above is that the commanding officer does not have control over his or her people and is unfit to be promoted. While there are specially trained units to investigate allegations of misconduct, the commanding officer, generally a person with no legal training, is left to decide the merits of the accusations. This often makes it difficult for victims to receive justice.

The victims are often forced to continue working with the people who have assaulted them, so the simple act of coming to work each day becomes retraumatizing. And for many victims, there is no way out: Their request for reassignment is often denied. All too often the victims decide to end their military career, sometimes jeopardizing their future pension.

While in the past victims were told to drop the charges and let it be, today more and more women and men who have been raped, sodomized, and sexually harassed while on active duty are stepping forward and speaking out.

Because of these issues, sexual assault has a larger impact in the symptomatology of PTSD (and mental health) than even combat duty. Victims of military sexual trauma often lead a life of isolation, disconnected from their emotions and numbed to life. They can have difficulty trusting others, not only those in positions of authority but when it comes to intimate relationships as well. Frequently, the victims have a long history of self-medicating with drugs or alcohol in an attempt to cope with daily life.

The most common complaints from these men and women are: emotional disengagement or flatness; difficulty with attention, concentration, and memory; and strong emotional and physical reactions to triggers; hypervigilance; trouble sleeping; nightmares; dissociation; difficulties with hierarchical environments (making it difficult to work); difficulties in social settings; alcohol and drug use; self-harm (e.g., cutting); eating disorders; revictimization; and suicidal thoughts or behavior.[10]

❖

Kate was 44 when she came to the Center. An intelligent woman with a wicked sense of humor, she had joined the Marines right out of high school just before the first Gulf War, and her father, a former Marine himself, was really proud. She had gotten through boot camp with no difficulty and had gone on to train as an air traffic controller. For six months, she had been stationed at a Marine Corps air base and loved the work she was doing.

In 1991, Kate's entire battalion was deployed to the Middle East aboard an aircraft carrier, and she found herself working 12-hour shifts, sometimes seven days a week, with the eight men in her unit. They joked, made coffee for each other, shared problems with boyfriends and girlfriends, and, as Kate explained, felt just like family.

Late one evening, Kate was making her way to the restroom when she was grabbed from behind and pulled into a tiny closet. Duct tape was placed across her mouth and her hands were taped behind her back. She kicked and squirmed, but it was no use — within minutes she had been stripped of all her clothing and brutally raped by Jake, one of the men she worked with. When he was finished with her, he spit on her and said, "Don't think for a moment that you are as good as we are," untaped her wrists, and stormed out of the closet, leaving her to get dressed and get back

Military Sexual Trauma

to work. She still had five hours on duty that night.

The next morning Kate went to the highest-ranking female officer on board ship. This officer filed a report and told Kate she would keep her posted as to what happened next. Weeks went by, and Kate heard nothing. Finally Kate returned to ask the female officer what was being done about her assault. Kate reminded her that she had to work with this man every day, and told her that she could no longer sleep at night, was starting to have panic attacks whenever she was on duty with her attacker, and was losing weight because she could no longer eat, as she felt nauseated almost all the time.

Kate was told that her attacker had been interviewed and had said that the sex they had was consensual, that he had done nothing wrong, and that it was her word against his. She was told that no action would be taken. The commanding officer had decided on this course of action.

After six months at sea, locked in with her attacker, Kate finally returned to her home port, and she went to her family doctor, who immediately hospitalized her for symptoms of acute PTSD. By this time Kate could no longer sleep more than two hours and was having nightmares when she did sleep. She was imagining she was seeing her attacker whenever she was in a crowd, was angry all the time, and was contemplating suicide. She felt no one cared about what had happened to her, and, worst of all, that no one was helping her cope with the aftermath.

After release from the hospital and six months of medication, Kate arrived at my office no longer suicidal and able to sleep. She wanted to work through the PTSD symptoms. After eight months of therapy, using mental imagery and other modalities, Kate decided to leave the military and go back to school to train as a nurse, which had always been her dream.

IMAGERY EXERCISES FOR SEXUAL TRAUMA

Sticks of Light

Intention: To turn darkness into light.
Frequency: Morning, evening and before bed for 21 days.

Close your eyes and breathe out three times slowly. See and sense the 10, 000 sticks of light being raised against the darkness. Know that the demons have fled. Breathe out and open your eyes.

Cloak

Intention: To eliminate the feelings of danger.
Frequency: Do as needed.

Close your eyes and breathe out three times slowly. Wrap yourself in your cloak of invisibility, knowing that you are safe from danger. Breathe out and open your eyes.

The Lake of Tears

Intention: To cleanse away pain.
Frequency: Morning, evening, and before bed for 21 days.

Close your eyes and breathe out three times slowly. Imagine a lake in the sky. See that it is a lake of tears. Breathe out. A drop of water falls from a cloud onto the lake of tears; this added drop is a tipping point, stirring up pain within you. Breathe out. Imagine the pain or difficulty shooting out from you as a flaming ball falling into the lake of tears. Breathe out. See and know what the flaming ball becomes when it falls into the lake. See the transformed ball of fire emerge from the lake. Breathe out. See your soul leave your body to hunt in the sky for the now transformed ball. Breathe out. See and sense what is happening around you and have your soul reenter your body. Breathe out and open your eyes.

Challenger Deep

Intention: To bury your deepest secrets.
Frequency: Morning, evening, and before bed for 21 days.

Close your eyes and breathe out three times slowly. See a box in front of you. In this box, place all the secrets that you have held deeply within yourself. Breathe out one time. Close the box and seal it tightly. Tie a boulder to it and throw it into the deepest part of the ocean called the Challenger Deep. Breathe out one time.

Know that these secrets are no longer tethered to you. Breathe out and open your eyes.

Rainbow Staircase

Intention: To become whole.
Frequency: Twice a day, morning and night, for 21 days.

Close your eyes and breathe out, counting backward from three to one, each outbreath being a new number you see in front of you. See the number one as tall and bright. Step inside the one, becoming one with yourself, returning to your inner space and your deep, inner rhythm. Now see a staircase of seven steps, each step a color of the rainbow: red, orange, yellow, green, blue, indigo, and violet. Breathe out, and start to ascend this rainbow staircase. See and sense the resonance or sound of each color. Notice how each color moves and fills your body with its cleansing light. When you reach the seventh step, leap to the heavens and plunge into the source of the rainbow, immersing yourself in its clear, pure radiance. Breathe out. Now descend the rainbow staircase, carrying this light back into your daily life. See your soul shining forth in the world once again. Breathe out and open your eyes, knowing you are whole and complete.

Golden Lasso

Intention: To be heard and acknowledged.
Frequency: Morning, evening, and before bed for 21 days.

Close your eyes and breathe out three times slowly. Take a golden lasso, and with a strong right arm, throw the lasso over the people who have ignored your input, response, or feedback. Tie or pin them against a golden fence, so they can only move their heads. Now that you have their attention, using your right index finger, tell them exactly what needs to be said. See them shaking their heads in agreement. Breathe out and open your eyes.

The Inside Observer

Intention: To find peace and communion.
Frequency: Once in the morning for seven days.

Close your eyes and breathe out three times slowly. Wash or sweep away: someone who is disturbing you; some inside imbalance; some regret; some physical ache that you don't know how to get rid of; or some event you cannot forget.

Breathe out one time and hear the voice of your higher self. This voice rests in your heart. It quells anxiety and takes away the pain of uncertainty, insecurity, impotence, resentment, rage, and pessimism. Breathe out one time and feel how direct communion with your higher self brings peace and confidence to your heart.

Breathe out one time. See how the victory of your heart over strife leads you into the light. Breathe out and open your eyes.

The Garden of Eden

Intention: To cleanse and purify yourself.
Frequency: Morning, evening, and before bed for 21 days.

Close your eyes and breathe out three times slowly. Imagine yourself leaving your home and going out into the street (descending a staircase or elevator, if you normally do). Leave the street and see yourself descending into a valley, meadow, or garden. Go to the center of it. Find there a golden feather duster, a witch broom, or a hand rake (depending on your preference or the degree of cleansing you need). With this tool, quickly clean yourself thoroughly, from top to bottom, including your extremities. See how you look and feel, knowing that you have cleaned away all the dead cells from the outside of your body and all the gloom and confusion from the inside. Put down the tool, and breathe out one time slowly.

Hear the sound of a flowing stream or brook coming from your right. Go there and kneel by its edge. Take the fresh-flowing, crystal-clear cool water in your cupped hands and splash it over your face, knowing that you are washing away all the impurities from the outside of your body. Feel and sense yourself refreshed, tingling, energized, and more awake.

Breathe out one time. Getting up from the stream, find a tree at the edge of the meadow. Sit under a tree that has branches filled with abundant verdant-green leaves. With your back against the trunk, breathe in the pure oxygen that the leaves emit in the form of a blue-golden light. Breathe out the carbon dioxide waste as gray smoke, which the leaves take up to convert into oxygen. See and sense the oxygen given off by the leaves. Sense the oxygen entering the trunk of the tree and then flowing to your body through your pores. Create a cycle with the tree, breathing as one with it. Let your fingers and toes curl into the earth like roots and draw up its energy. Stay there for a long moment, taking in what you need. Then get up and see how you look and feel.

Keep this image and feelings for yourself as you leave the garden and return to your street and home by the same route you came. Sense and feel yourself back in the chair. Breathe out and open your eyes.

The Orchid
(*For women*)

Intention: To purify and resanctify the vagina.
Frequency: Morning, evening, and before bed for 21 days.

Close your eyes and breathe out three times. Find yourself in a large, open field of green grass. Stretching your fingers toward the sun, see the sun's rays permeating your palms and fingers, filling them with rays of light. In your right hand, you have five mini hands, one on the tip of each finger. On your left hand, you have five mini eyes, one at the tip of each finger, each emitting light. Now, become very small and enter a vanilla orchid. Smell the vital fragrance of vanilla. With one of your right mini hands, take some vanilla beans with you. Leave the orchid and enter your vagina, using your five mini eyes to see your way clearly. Survey the vaginal walls (and womb). In one of your mini hands have a small golden brush with which you clean away any remnants of the physical toxins and emotional residue that are embedded in your cells. Clean the area thoroughly (remember that you are looking carefully at what you are doing all the time with your five eyes). With your small hand containing the vanilla beans, plant the beans in the areas where you have removed the cells and toxic residue, and with your five eyes see beautiful white orchids growing out from the vaginal walls. In another small hand have a golden watering can filled with pure rainwater and use it to water the orchids, watching the petals unfolding, smelling the aromatic fragrance of vanilla. Know that the vagina is healing perfectly. Leave the vagina, taking any waste materials with you. Exit from your body by the way you entered, and with your mini hands, throw any waste material *behind* you, putting the past behind you as well. Then, growing to your usual size, hold your hands and palms up to the sun, and let the mini eyes and hands retract into your palms to be stored for future use. Breathe out and open your eyes.

Diamonds on the Soles of Your Feet

Intention: To restore your self-image and self-worth.
Frequency: Morning, evening, and before bed for 21 days.

Close your eyes and breathe out slowly three times. See, sense, and feel yourself removing your old worn-out shoes, knowing that you are removing your "walking blues."

To your right, find a new pair of shoes embedded with diamonds in their soles.

See, sense, and feel the sparkling light of the diamonds spreading up through and around you, creating an aura of well-being. With these shoes on your feet, walk into a new future. What do you find there? How do you feel? Keep this feeling for yourself. Breathe out and open your eyes.

CHAPTER 17
Life Plan and Stopping Exercises: Using Your Will

Will is our life force impulse that enables us to make choices and take action. We each have a will, and it is reflected in the choices we make each day, all day, when we arise, get up, dress, go to work, or engage in a mental practice such as mental imagery. When we give our will a direction, we have an intention or aim that manifests our creations. And as we stated earlier in this book, intention is an aim toward something, without consideration of a goal or outcome.

We use our will actively to think, feel, and act in non-habitual ways. Two techniques of will are called *Life Plan* and *Stopping*. Presented here in simplified forms, both can be used to curb addictions and distressing emotions and traits.[11]

LIFE PLAN

In Life Plan, you pick a disturbing characteristic or trait and convert it to its *opposite*. By practicing or remembering the opposite tendency, you come into balance by uniting these opposite

Life Plan and Stopping Exercises: Using Your Will

traits. In a sense you are uprooting a trait and planting its opposite in your garden of consciousness through repeated use of will.

Pick out a characteristic you wish to change. Now close your eyes and ask yourself what new (not necessary opposite) characteristic would emerge if the distressing tendency or trait were cut off. You may receive an answer as a word, image, sensation, or feeling. Every time the disturbing trait comes up in your daily life, stop for a moment and replace it with a new trait, picking a color that connects the two traits as a reminder to shift from one tendency to the other. It is as simple as that — the whole process takes just a few seconds.

Here's an example. Take the trait of *anxiety*. Let's say that you recognized the word *balance* as the opposite (or new trait) that would emerge if you had no *anxiety*. You ask yourself what color connects these two traits and may spontaneously see the color *blue* as the connecting color. On day one, tell yourself that you are going to change *anxiety* to *balance,* and your reminder will be the color *blue* (shown as gray in the illustration on the next page). Then, during the next 21 days, whenever you become aware that you are feeling anxious, you *stop* for an instant and close your eyes. You see the word *anxiety* and a *blue line* coming from the word *to* a center point and going across to its opposite, *balance*. At that moment, you say the word *balance* silently, then open your eyes. This repeated reminder to shift from anxiety to balance helps you break the habit of anxiety. On a physiological basis, you are rewiring your neural networks.

```
         BALANCE  ◄─────●─────  ANXIETY
```

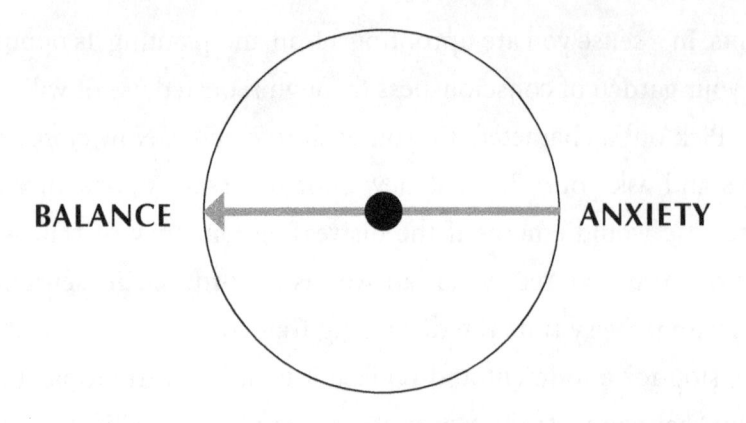

At the end of 21 days, stop for seven days. At the end of the seven-day rest period, assess whether you have imprinted the new quality. If you have overcome habitual anxiety, choose another characteristic and begin work anew. If, at the end of the seven days, you decide that the imprinting has not taken, then continue to work on that trait for two more cycles of 21 days, resting seven days between cycles.

Take another example — *addiction* to alcohol. Simply close your eyes and ask yourself what opposite characteristic would emerge if the addiction were cut off. Let us say you receive an image of yourself *jogging* on a sunny spring day. Now ask yourself what color links these two traits. Let's say you discover or imaginally see the color of bright yellow. On day one, tell yourself that you are going to change addiction to jogging, and your reminder will be the color yellow. Then when you become aware of a desire to drink, you *stop* for an instant and close your eyes. You see the word *addiction*, and the yellow line coming from that word to the center point and going across to its opposite, *jogging*. At that moment, you say the word *jogging* silently (or see an image of jogging), then

Life Plan and Stopping Exercises: Using Your Will

open your eyes. At the end of 21 days, stop for seven days. At the end of the seven-day rest period, assess. In addition, you may wish to physically jog each day to reinforce this change.

As you can see from this last example of addiction/jogging, when you cut off a tendency, what emerges as its opposite tendency may not be a simple opposite or antonym. Here again, logic doesn't dictate, so trust what you discover.

Here are some other tips:
- Work on only one characteristic at a time.
- After awhile you may not need a color to shift from one tendency to its opposite.
- If you forget to do the Life Plan and lapse into the habitual trait, do the process when you remember.

STOPPING EXERCISES

Stopping exercises are a reversing technique to break addictive habits. Like imagery, these exercises are quick and easy to do. In stopping exercises, you momentarily stop yourself before acting — or not — on an addictive craving. The principle is to alter momentarily the rhythm of the habitual addictive activity. It can also be used to delay a particular emotional pattern of reactivity, such as shouting or hitting when you find yourself becoming angry. Such stopping provides a short shock to the system, which stimulates the body to respond in a new way while waking you up mentally. Pick only one addictive activity (or habitual emotional response) to work on for 21 days, such as:

- Smoking a cigarette or joint
- Drinking coffee, beer, wine, or hard liquor
- Angry outbursts
- Bingeing or compulsive eating (or purging after eating)

Each stopping exercise has an intention. If you wish to stop smoking, you would hesitate for an instant and recall your intention — by saying "no smoking" or seeing yourself throwing away the cigarette — before you remove the match from the box, or before you strike the match, or as you place the match at the end of the cigarette. The stopping action lasts only an instant. Whether you complete the action or not is up to you. In curbing your tendency to lash out and shout when angry, you would hesitate for an instant before the act and recall your intention — by saying "no shouting" or seeing an imaginal "stop" sign, or seeing yourself turning away, or singing your response, for example. Whatever follows is accepted without judgment. With eating, you stop for a moment as you bring the fork or spoon to your mouth; with purging, you take a moment and stop before purging. Stopping is an ongoing practice that requires that you remember to do it consistently for 21 days then stop for seven days. If you feel your intention requires more work, resume the stopping exercise for another two cycles of 21 days. If, during the course of practicing stopping, you forget to carry it out, don't berate or criticize yourself. Simply accept this fact and carry on with your practice.

CHAPTER 18

For the Families of Vets

Being in combat creates many hardships for both active military personnel and for veterans. We have seen that war can create a state of mind that can endure for years, decades, even a lifetime. And what we don't always consider is that when military personnel or veterans are suffering, their families are generally having a difficult time as well.

❖

Mark was a Vietnam veteran who had a successful travel business and had raised two sons with his wife, Peg. When we decided to start a class for family members of veterans who had been diagnosed with PTSD, Peg and her two adult children were the first to sign up. During the first class meeting, we went around the room and each family member shared how the PTSD of their loved one had made their own life challenging. Peg began to cry. "I just can't believe this," she said, looking from face to face at the other people around her. "I can't believe it." Then her son Aaron said, "All these years we thought Dad was an angry person, a person who didn't love us enough because he would never come to watch us play football or attend our school plays. Now I know why. He couldn't stand to be in the crowds, and he was too ashamed to tell us." "Yeah," said Courtney, a high school senior. "Mom always thinks the worst stuff is going to happen to me because her life in Iraq was so scary, I guess."

"I never knew," said Matt, "that Dad has so much trouble going to the air show, which I love, because the noise triggers him and he is back in the war. He goes with me because he loves me, but he suffers the whole time. I'm not gonna ask him to do it anymore."

IMAGERY EXERCISES FOR THE FAMILY

Browsing through the book, you may find many exercises in the grief, depression, anger, and insomnia sections that may resonate with issues that family members typically face. Feel free to use them. In addition, included are several exercises for relaxation, stress, fear, feeling burdened, and money worries.

Sand Salutation Exercise
(*To relax and reinvigorate*)
- See page 42 -

For Families of Vets

The White Silk Cape

Intention: For protection and overcoming fear.
Frequency: As needed.

With eyes closed or opened, breathe out three times slowly. See a white silk cape in front of you. Put it on and fly high above whatever you fear. What do you experience? Know that the fear has dissipated. Breathe out and open your eyes.

The Garden of Eden
(*For self-renewal*)
- See page 150 -

Blue Sky Umbrella
(*For anxiety and protection*)
- See page 74 -

Atlas Shrugged

Intention: To feel unburdened.
Frequency: Morning, evening, and before bed for 21 days.

Close your eyes and breathe out three times slowly. See, sense, and feel yourself as Atlas holding the world on your shoulders. Now remove from your shoulders the burdens that are weighing you down, putting them **behind you**, seeing yourself grow a hundred times taller than you are. Take note of your feelings and any physical sensations. Breathe out and open your eyes.

Breathing as One
(For couples or partners)

Intention: To repair communication between partners.
Frequency: Twice a day, in the morning and before bed, for seven, 14, or 21 days.

> *Note:* Do this exercise for the first time together. Thereafter, each person can do it by themselves.

Close your eyes and breathe out three times slowly. See and sense yourself standing at the base of a large, tall tree, facing the tree. Your partner is standing on the other side of the tree, facing the tree as well. Sense and feel yourself firmly grounded on the earth, drawing energy from it. Sense yourself breathing deeply and rhythmically, feeling the tree breathing in harmony with you. Sense your partner's breathing coming into rhythm with yours so that you both are breathing as one with the tree. Now see both your and your partner's arms and legs growing longer, extending to embrace one another while growing taller and taller until your heads both reach the crown of the tree. Know that you are growing as one. Keep this feeling of oneness. Breathe out and open your eyes.

Stress Without Distress

Intention: To remove distress.

Frequency: Once in the morning for 21 days. Prerecord the exercises or have someone read it to you.

1. Close your eyes and breathe out three times slowly. See yourself feeding powerful giants. Breathe out and open your eyes.
2. Close your eyes and breathe out two times. See yourself making friends with hostile beings. Breathe out and open your eyes.
3. Close your eyes and breathe out two times. See yourself knotting the head of a snake. Breathe out and open your eyes.
4. Close your eyes and breathe out three times. See yourself jumping on the back of a traveling dragon. Breathe out and open your eyes.
5. Close your eyes and breathe out one time. See yourself calling forth the hidden inhabitants of a cavern. Breathe out and open your eyes.
6. Close your eyes and breathe out two times. See yourself facing ghosts in an old castle. Breathe out and open your eyes.

7. Close your eyes and breathe out one time. See yourself finding a powerful soul in a catacomb. Breathe out and open your eyes.
8. Close your eyes and breathe out three times. See yourself leading a strange animal into a deep forest. Breathe out and open your eyes.
9. Close your eyes and breathe out one time. Look at a target that you have overshot. What is the proper action? Do you need a helper? Breathe out and open your eyes.
10. Close your eyes and breathe out one time. Look at a bird soaring upward when it is safer for the bird to remain low. What do you experience? Breathe out and open your eyes.
11. Close your eyes and breathe out one time. See how you have to struggle with the changing tide to fulfill your true self. Breathe out and open your eyes.
12. Close your eyes and breathe out one time. See why, after the struggle, we can then be still. Breathe out and open your eyes.
13. Close your eyes and breathe out one time. Know when it is good to speak and when it is good to remain silent. Breathe out and open your eyes.
14. Close your eyes and breathe out one time. Know that whatever is going on in our society, you need not be impatient nor need you surrender. Breathe out and open your eyes.
15. Close your eyes and breathe out. See that what is hastily made is quickly destroyed. Breathe out and open your eyes.
16. Close your eyes and breathe out one time. Looking into

clear, quiet, calm water, see what you wish to see. Breathe out and open your eyes.
17. Close your eyes and breathe out one time. Looking into clear, calm water, change your appearance to what you would like it to be. Breathe out and open your eyes.

Net Worth Exercise

Intention: To increase income.
Frequency: Each morning for 21 days. If desired, repeat for two more cycles of 21 days, stopping for seven days between cycles.

Close your eyes and breathe out three times slowly. See yourself hurling a fine golden net into the cosmos, catching for yourself the sustenance you need. Breathe out one time, and bring the net back down to you. Open it and remove and keep what you have brought down for yourself. Breathe out and open your eyes.

Note: Remember not to be concerned or focused on the result. An intention is an aim, not a fixed goal.

UNFOLDING THE DAY: DIRECTING YOUR WILL TO BENEFIT YOURSELF

This exercise has several parts — imagery exercises and a physical exercise — that are done at different times of the day. Do it in cycles of 21 days, stopping seven days between cycles.

1) Imagery Exercise Upon Awakening

Intention: To set the day in order.
Frequency: Once in the morning, before starting your day.

Close your eyes and breathe out three times slowly. See the day quickly unfolding from morning until bedtime, flowing from one activity to the next. See yourself at ease, mastering each task, focused, calm, and relaxed. Breathe out and open your eyes.

2) Cleaning a Physical Space

Intention: To cleanse yourself inside or out; to put yourself in order.
Frequency: Once in the morning, before starting your day.

Physically clean a space such as your bathroom or kitchen sink with a paper towel or cloth for a few seconds, knowing that as you do this you are cleaning yourself inside and out as well.

3) Connecting to Nature

Intention: To connect to nature and the rhythm of life.
Frequency: Once a day for several seconds.

When you leave the house, stop for a moment and merge or become one with something in nature. Breathe out. For example, feel yourself as one with a tree, bush, flower. Sense and feel its connection to the earth and to the sky. Sense and feel its inner stillness and calm. If you are housebound, go to a window and connect with something you see in nature outside or even with a houseplant.

4) Imagery Exercise Before Going to Bed

(Reversing the Day)
- See page 97 for more details -

Intention: To correct any errors of the day.
Frequency: Once a day before bed.

While lying in bed, quickly review the day in reverse order from your last activity before bed all the way back to your first activity in the morning. Imaginally correct any disturbing events or conversations. You may find that you fall asleep before you complete the exercise.

CHAPTER 19
Creating Your Own Exercises

After working with the imagery in this book, you are now able to create your own imagery. In fact, you may already have noticed that you naturally modified or tweaked the imagery you have done. Imagery that comes from within you is very powerful. Here are eight pointers from Dr. Epstein to keep in mind when creating your own imagery exercises.[12]

1) Always start with your point of trouble. We saw in Chapter 2 that Austin wanted to overcome his inability to go to church. This was his point of trouble — the immediate problem. This approach works for any ailment.

2) Any image you find is right for you. It is important not to judge or otherwise question the apparent sense the image makes. Do not try to interpret it or figure it out. You may find useful imagery coming to you from your night dreams or the way you talk about your problems. For example, if you say that you are in "the pit of despair," create an imagery exercise where you see yourself climbing out of the pit.

Creating Your Own Exercises

3) Trust that you will be able to make use of your image. Anything can happen in imagination, and you can bring anything with you to help you in your imagery. For example, you may bring a light, a cape, a golden broom, etc.

4) Imagery re-regulates our body rhythms. These rhythms are affected by outer disturbances, such as climactic changes, as well as inner disturbances. When we are sick or feeling imbalanced, our body rhythms can become too fast or too slow. For example, a state of anxiety can produce a heart rhythm that is too fast or too slow. In using imagery, watch the rhythms of your disturbance. The general rule is to use the opposite of what you struggle with. If you are suffering from a "too fast" condition such as stress, use quieting imagery to slow down the system, and vice versa. If you are in a state of "too slow" a condition, such as depression, use imagery that speeds up the system, such as imagining yourself running in a red jogging suit.

5) You can apply a paradoxical approach to the problem you are working with. That means that you apply what makes the least sense in a given situation, something that does not seem necessarily logical. For example, when you are feeling pain, your tendency is to want to turn and flee from it. The paradox here is to do exactly the opposite. Join the pain, shake hands with the pain, become the pain. By accepting the pain and not resisting it, it loses power.

6) Inner guides sometimes appear when you do imagery.

None of the exercises in this volume require an inner guide, but if you should encounter one, do not hesitate to ask the guide to help you. You can call on this inner guide in your imaginal experiences or in your everyday waking life experience (much like calling on a guardian angel or a saint for assistance).

7) Whatever you discover for yourself in the imaginal reality, whatever answer you may find, whatever instruction you may receive, you need to carry it out in your everyday activities as a lived experience to gain its benefits. *You need to manifest your inner belief as an outer experience.* For example, one person discovered the Ten Commandments in her imagery work. She then bought a large gold charm depicting the Ten Commandments and wore it around her neck. She subsequently noticed that the recklessness she had been experiencing in her life quieted down. A young man was working on addictions and saw an amethyst stone in his imagery. This stone was known to the ancient Greeks to protect one from drinking. The client purchased a small amethyst stone to remind himself to stop binge drinking. *What you find in your imagery work are pictorial instructions telling you what you need.*

8) Most importantly, do not compare yourself to anyone else. It is not important that you get better faster than another person with a similar problem. Your only focus should be on yourself, on establishing your own health.

CHAPTER 20

Choosing to Live Well

Mr. Johnson, age 77, came to the Vet Center in a wheelchair. He had been unable to walk independently after receiving cancer treatments two years before. What he wanted more than anything, he told me, was to be able to walk the short block to his mailbox. We worked together to create an imagery exercise to achieve this aim. Three weeks later, after Mr. Johnson had done the exercise three times daily, he walked into my office using a walker. He smiled broadly as he described how two days ago he had suddenly been able to stand up and then walk. He stated that he wanted to move beyond the walker and walk with a cane. Four weeks later, when I went to greet him in the waiting room to escort him to my office, I was delighted to see him stand up using only a cane and slowly walk beside me down the corridor.

This reaffirmed what I have witnessed through my work in this field over two decades: The impossible often becomes possible when working with mental imagery. Through the simplest of exercises we can shift our physical, mental, and emotional suffering to free ourselves so we are no longer victims. Instead of living in a body that contains a mind filled with darkness and despair —

often manifesting as a kind of living death — we instead live with the knowledge of possibility and change.

We can break the cycle of suffering and see our situation from a new perspective. The activity of seeing anew and thereby taking action is what this book is really about. When we take action — both through imagery and physical activity — we are no longer victims of injury, pain, and fear. We become free of the past, and in the present moment we are able to see things as they are. When we correct past errors of thinking and doing, we are born anew. This is real freedom.

During this process, we learn to become our own authority, we become confident in what is taking place in our body and mind as we grow into healing. We learn not to think about what should be, but about what is and how we can learn from that. In this way, we choose life. In thus choosing, we reverse what has grown stale and unmovable, changing it into what is full of life and light, ready to meet life head-on to reach our full potential.

Here are four exercises that you can do anytime to remind yourself that you are moving toward freedom.

IMAGERY EXERCISES FOR LIVING WELL

Cleansing the Heart

Intention: To feel satisfied and contented.
Frequency: Once in the morning for 21 days.

Close your eyes and breathe out three times slowly. Open your chest between the breasts. Gently take out your heart. How does it look? Clean off or remove anything in or on the heart that needs to be cleansed away. Then, see what comes out of your heart. Use what emerges to renew your heart and feel contented. Gently put your heart back in your chest and seal your chest up once more. Breathe out and open your eyes.

Reimagining Yourself

Intention: To reshape yourself and repair a poor self-image.
Frequency: Once in the morning for 21 days

Close your eyes and breathe out three times slowly. See yourself in front of a mirror. Now, with the index finger of your dominant hand, reshape and remold your image in the mirror — adding what you want, removing what you no longer want or need. When you are satisfied with your new self-image, push the image to the right, out of the mirror with your right hand. Breathe out and open your eyes.

Life and Light

Intention: To live lightly.
Frequency: Once in the morning for 21 days.

Close your eyes and breathe out three times slowly. See, sense, and feel yourself becoming moderate and obtaining balance in all dimensions of living. See yourself setting aside a half-minute twice a day for quieting imagery. See yourself reducing the frequency of stress in your life.

Breathe out and see, sense, and feel that you are now more able to accept your physical and emotional limitations.

Breathe out and see that you can break the spiral of stress by balancing work and play.

Breathe out and see how being less serious can break the stress cycle.

Breathe out and see how you have fun when you are light-hearted.

Breathe out and see yourself gaining perspective when an intense or painful scene is happening.

Breathe out and know that you can use imagery or a healthy outlet — walking, gardening, drinking a glass of water slowly, washing your hands slowly to deal with stressful situations.

Breathe out and see yourself smiling a true smile. Relax and sense the muscles of a true smile.

Breathe out three times. Sense, feel, and know that life is your first teacher and your medium for self-expression by means of change and growth.

Breathe out one time. Live how seriousness is making you heavy, while your inner images make you light and alive. Breathe out and open your eyes.

The Mummy

Intention: To live freely.
Frequency: Once in the morning for 21 days.

Close your eyes and breathe out three times slowly. Imagine you are a mummy that is in a sarcophagus (a stone container), in a cellar, within a cave in a mountain. You are still living after thousands of years, but you can only move the little finger of each hand. You manage to find the end of the bandage wrapped around your body. You unwrap it and find you can unwind it into a small ball that grows larger as you undo the bandage. Every minute you feel freer and more alive until you've entirely unrolled the bandage. You now have a large ball in your hand. You try to move, and you find you can do it easily. You get up out of the sarcophagus. You are in a very nice cave, where the walls are painted with ancient pictures. It is superb, but you have no time to examine it, as you are eager to see what's going on outside. You manage to go out of the cave and realize it is night, a very starry night.

Breathe out one time. You look at the stars and throw the ball of bandages that was wrapped around you to the stars. At that moment, you feel entirely free, and the ball turns into a star. In the starlight, you walk downhill and arrive in the town where you live, in front of your house. Dawn now approaches, and you see the sun begin to rise. As you enter your home, know you are free — not only liberated, but free. You are both the same and different. You have made great progress in a short time. Breathe out and open your eyes.

CHAPTER 21

Notes For Healthcare Professionals

Mental Imagery as a Therapeutic Modality

For many years, healthcare professionals working with both active-duty American military personnel and veterans were encouraged to use only conventional, evidence-based treatments for war trauma, such as medication, talk therapy, and biofeedback. It was believed that positive results could be measured only by assessing outcomes using quantitative methods. But over time, it became clear that many active-duty military personnel and veterans resisted these methods or found them only partially effective.

Many mental health practitioners started looking for new ways and approaches to help clients improve their day-to-day functioning and overall well-being. The Department of Defense began investigating clinically based qualitative methods such as the use of mindbody medicine to treat patients with head trauma and PTSD.[13] Mindbody medicine, broadly defined, is a holistic model of health that considers the complete human being as an integrative whole made up of physical, mental, emotional, social (relational), and moral/spiritual dimensions.[14] From a mindbody perspective, *the subjective experience of self cannot be known through the objective world.* As Nobel prize winner of physics Erwin Schrödinger explained, the subject can come to know itself only through subjective means. From this point of view, the subject coming to know itself through objective means is scientifically unsound. Alternative avenues of healing, such as mental imagery, meditation, hypnosis, and somatic therapies, are all subjective means to know the self. This exploration of self through these subjective disciplines can be a key to healing PTSD in conjunction with conventional medical therapies.

Some of the most recent and powerful ways of understanding the brain and its functions have come from studies seeking to discover what causes the brain to regenerate after it has been injured. Especially since the Iraq and Afghanistan wars, questions have arisen about how best to treat traumatic brain injury (in its mild form known as concussion). Scientists have discovered that while healing from this type of injury can remain stubbornly elusive, more can generally be done to reverse injury than had previously been thought. The ability of the brain to create new pathways when others have been blocked is called *neuroplasticity*.[15]

Part of this new way of looking at healing derives from the mid–20th century work of Lev Vygotsky, a Soviet psychologist. In his experiments with Russian children, he discovered that learning best happens in activity.[16] When we engage in interactive work — with another person or even with a text — what we learn is retained longer and is better understood. Vygotsky coined the term *zones of proximal development* to describe this ideal approach to teaching and learning. Mental imagery is a type of internal interactive work where we turn work into play.

Medical science is slowly affirming the efficacy of these holistic healing practices by better understanding the neurophysiology at play in acute and chronic stress. Researchers at the Stanford University School of Medicine discovered the physiological underpinnings of how slow and smooth breathing induces calm, while fast and uncontrolled breathing induces tension. A cluster of 175 neurons in the brain stem collectively called the *pacemaker for breathing*, monitor (rather than regulate) respiration and relay this information to the brain's locus coeruleus (or blue nucleus). The coeruleus, a small ganglion of neurons, connects to all areas of the brain and drives our arousal system — from waking us from sleep, keeping us alert, to triggering anxiety and distress. Thus, it now appears that breathing plays a key role in arousal and emotion.[17] When we breathe out long, slow exhalations — as we do in mental imagery, meditation, yogic breathing, hypnosis, and other mindful practices that include breath work — we are calming ourselves. Additionally, long, slow exhalations eliminate not only carbon dioxide but also the chronic stress hormone peripheral noradrenaline.[18]

Researchers have long known that memories are malleable. In PTSD, imagery plays a large part in memory distortion and amplification to somatically fortify the memories of traumatic events.[19] These events can be encapsulated into one core memory that acts as a hologram for all the traumatic events witnessed. Hence, war veterans and active-duty combatants often report only a single repeated traumatic memory, flashback, or nightmare. In our treatment modality, we can take these remembered core traumatic events and actively reverse them. Just as the mind can trick us into

Notes For Healthcare Professionals

responding to events that have not happened in objective reality, we can use the same mechanism to trick the mind into reversing, replacing, or retracing these memories with more functional, less reactive ones. This last technique is described in Appendix B for healthcare professionals.

Finally, research has shown that a regular practice of mental imagery increases physiological coherence — the orderly and harmonious synchronization of bodily systems — such as the heart, respiration, and blood pressure rhythms.[20] In sum, mental imagery enhances physiological well-being as it increases one's sense of emotional and mental well-being.

CHAPTER 22

For Clinicians

Techniques to Reverse Nightmares, Flashbacks, and Intrusive Memories

People heal at different rates, and at different points in their lives they are able to engage in mental imagery on different levels. This section provides additional imagery tools for clinicians whose clients are ready to go more deeply into direct healing from the core traumatic event. In these exercises, the client returns to the pivotal point of the nightmare, flashback, or intrusive memory and reverses or corrects it.

Through my work at the Vet Center, I found that some PTSD sufferers could not immediately reverse the most profound traumatic memories without assistance. Recalling the trauma, even in a therapeutic setting, was sometimes re-traumatizing. Thus, I developed the strategy followed throughout this book of stripping off the layers of hyperreactivity through short imagery exercises. In this way, the trauma fades bit by bit from the forefront of the sufferers' mind and body, allowing them to function more effectively and joyously in the world. This strategy also allowed me to meet people where they were — helping them tackle the day-to-day problems they faced, such as driving, anxiety, anger management, fear, grief, guilt, pain, etc.

For Clinicians

By chipping away at the outer manifestations of the trauma, some clients are ready and able to imaginally retrace the past. In this type of reversing imagery exercise, the clinician acts as a guide for the client who repairs or corrects the memory. This process can take several seconds to a minute. Through the reversal or correction, the client replaces the pain of the event with a new possibility, attitude, or perception. When the client repeats the exercise alone, he or she need only imagine the corrected image, not the original disturbing image.

During my own healing process from war trauma, I worked in the same manner with my therapist, Dr. Epstein. The trauma I experienced occurred at Hebrew University in Jerusalem, where I was studying in the library. Suddenly there was a strong explosion, the library filled with smoke, and everyone ran for the exits. Once outside, I saw bodies of students lying all over the ground, some very badly wounded. A bomb had been placed by terrorists in the student café during lunchtime, when it was full of people.

For years, the image of these bodies had come to me in horrible dreams, and I wanted to be rid of these nightmares. Dr. Epstein had me correct the nightmare by returning to the most traumatic scene, where I walked through this field of bodies, from one side of the café to the other. At first, in reversing the nightmare imaginally, I could not even take a step and was frozen. As I repeated the imagery exercise, I was able to walk to the edge of where the bodies lay. After more weeks of practicing this exercise, I was able to walk across the area if I rose up and walked about five feet above the ground. Finally, after repeating this imagery exercise for some weeks, I was able to create an image of a path that went from one side of the café to the other where I could walk without fear or anxiety. The nightmares stopped, and I felt less anxious in general in my daily life.

I truly knew I had been healed when I visited Israel the following year. I returned to the very spot on the university campus where I had seen the bodies all those years ago. I felt neither fear nor anxiety. I had indeed succeeded in reversing the memory of this traumatic image, and I have not had a nightmare about this since; the correction has held up for over 30 years!

❖

CAUTION: These are strong exercises. Use them ONLY after a client has successfully used the imagery in this book to handle other issues.

Clinical Example of Correcting a Nightmare

Here is an example of a persistent nightmare from Dorothy, a Vietnam veteran. Dorothy was a competent and capable woman at work, and she had a family and a stable marriage. She came to me to work on her reactivity and volatility, which were triggered when she felt emotionally threatened. She described a recurrent nightmare she has had since childhood where she finds herself at the edge of an ocean on an overcast gray and gloomy day. A tidal wave is approaching the shore, and she is climbing up a cliff to escape it while it looms behind her.

For Clinicians

Acting as her guide, I have her return to the most significant image in the dream. I start by having her sit up in her chair, with her feet on the ground, eyes closed, counting backward from five to one, with a new outbreath on each number, with the one turning into a zero.

> *Note:* She is imaginally reversing time by counting backwards.

The zero then becomes a large mirror that she enters.

> *Note:* She is imaginally reversing space by entering the mirror.

She finds herself back at the shore, with the looming tidal wave about to break. Instead of running away, she chooses to dive into the depths of the tidal wave, into the calm sea below. There she meets Poseidon, Greek god of the sea, storms, and earthquakes. He gifts her his trident, a fork like spear through which he channels his power. She feels empowered, and discovers she is indeed his daughter.

Ready to return, she quickly retraces her path, ascending from the depth of the sea, back to the looming tidal wave, back to shore. I instruct her to then step out of the mirror, and looking into the mirror see the corrected image of herself holding the trident with Poseidon by her side. I then instruct her to imaginally push the image to the right out of the mirror, using her right hand.

> *Note*: the right is generally the future.

On the next outbreath, she sees the mirror turn into a one, and then counting forward from one to five, she imaginally sees each number with each new outbreath. At five, she feels herself back in the chair with her feet on the floor and then breathes out and opens her eyes. With her eyes open, I instruct her to look at the blank wall opposite her and to see the image of herself holding the trident.

I then instruct her, for the next 21 days to imaginally see herself each morning, for several seconds, as the daughter of Poseidon, with the trident in hand, knowing that she is able to channel her emotions through the trident and remain calm in the face of any perceived criticism.

Clinical Instructions for Correcting a Nightmare

As usual, instruct clients to sit up, with their feet on the floor and their arms on armrests of the chair or in their lap. Then give this special short breathing induction.

Initial Breathing Instructions

"Close your eyes and breathe out five times (i.e., five full respiratory cycles starting with an outbreath), counting backward from five to one, each outbreath being a new number. At one, see yourself very strong and tall, then breathe out again, and see the one becoming a zero and the zero growing in size and becoming a large mirror. Breathe out one time. Step into the mirror, and find

For Clinicians

yourself back in the most difficult point of the nightmare. Have with you whatever you need to help correct the event, or to conquer whatever is coming after you."[21]

> *Note:* For those clients who are uncomfortable stepping into an imaginal mirror, have them imaginally look into a mirror, seeing the nightmare scene, as they would view a movie.

Instructions During the Exercise

Ask the clients to describe in detail what is going on — who is there, where they are, what is going on, and how they are correcting the scene.

> *Note:* Clients should report in the present tense, and need to describe their perceptions, sensations, and feelings so you can guide and aid them as necessary in this realm, You can assist in guiding them if they are unable to imagine a new outcome.

After successfully correcting the dream, ask them to tell you how they look and feel. Then instruct them to step out of the mirror, look at the now corrected scene, and *imaginally* push it to the **right** [the future], out of the mirror, with their right hand.

> *Note*: On the initial go around, they may not be able to correct the scene to their full satisfaction, but as they continue to practice the exercise they may discover small changes each time in their ability to take control and master the nightmare. Each foray into the imaginal realm to correct the nightmare loosens the grip of the conditioning. However, if you find that they are unable to correct the image at all, or get overwhelmed, have them stop the imagery exercise and do several rounds of relaxed breathing (i.e., long slow exhalations through the mouth and normal inhalations through the nose). Instruct them to sense themselves back in the chair, with their feet firmly on the floor, and their focus back in the present moment.

Closing Breathing Instructions

Finish the imagery with these closing instructions that are the reverse of the induction:

"Now breathe out one time and see the mirror turning back into a one. Then count forward from one to five, with each new outbreath being a new number. At five, become aware of the chair supporting your back and your feet flat on the floor, and then slowly open your eyes. With your eyes open, if you can, see the image of the corrected event for a few seconds on the opposite wall, and then see the image fade."

For Clinicians

Follow-up

If clients are successful in reversing the event, or partially reversing the event, and feel confident of continuing this on their own, then instruct them as follows:

"Each morning, for the next 21 days, close your eyes, breathe out three times slowly, and imaginally go back into or view the *corrected* scene or event for a few seconds. If anything needs to be corrected, correct it. If nothing needs to be corrected, breathe out and open your eyes."

❖

Clinical Example of Correcting a Flashback or Intrusive Memory

Martin served in the first Iraq war as a driver. A quiet man, he now works in the computer field. He first came to see me describing symptoms of panic attacks while driving to and from work, as well as trouble sleeping through the night. After practicing the **Red Sea Parting** exercise for driving (page 30) and the **Perimeter Check** (page 94) for feeling safe at night, Martin reported that he felt calmer driving and was sleeping more soundly and for longer periods. Two months into our work together, I asked him if he could identify any disturbing flashbacks that he had. He replied that he had a persistent flashback of seeing the convoy ahead of him blow up.

I explained that painful memories like flashbacks operate in us as conditioned responses. To free ourselves of the effect of these painful memories, we need to correct them so that we are no longer locked in a conditioned stimulus-response cycle. I reminded him that in every stimulus-response there is a space of freedom between the stimulus and the response for us to choose a different response. When we insert a new response into our memory of the past, instead of activating the habitual response button, it activates the new memory, which now acts as the buffer between the stimulus and the habitual response. When the stimulus hits the buffer, we no longer get the habitual response, we get a brand-new one, and the new response ignites in us a new attitude, a new possibility, a new option, a new avenue of approach, a new habit. One memory can exemplify a whole range of similar experiences And like computer memory, our memories can be written over, deleting the old memory and freeing up internal space within us.[22]

During our session, I ask Martin to sit up, close his eyes, and breathe out three times slowly, counting backwards from three to one, seeing a new number with each outbreath. When he reaches one, I instruct him to breathe out one time and see the one become a zero that then turns into a round mirror. I then tell him to look into the mirror and see the disturbing flashback or memory. I tell him that he can have with him anything (or anyone) he needs to correct the memory. I ask Martin to describe what he sees, senses, and feels in the present tense. He describes the sound of the blast, watching the truck just ahead explode in flames, and seeing the burnt body of a fellow soldier lying on the ground. During the process, he reports that he is feeling the heat from the explosion and noticing the smell of gas and smoke, as well as his heart pounding. I ask him to correct the memory, reminding him that anything is possible in the realm of imagination. I ask him to describe the correction. With EYES STILL CLOSED, Martin relates

For Clinicians

his correction or repair of the memory: He sees the convoy leader signal that there is an IED ahead of them. The convoy trucks then line up in a formation, sprout wings, and fly over the IED to the home base. I tell him to breathe out one time and *to tell me how he looks and feels.* He senses his breath and his heart slowing down to a normal pace, and he sees himself and his comrades relaxed and laughing. His face is relaxed. He keeps his eyes **closed** while I tell him: *"You have lived again these now-corrected events with a different past and a new now. (See how you may become in one year from now, two years from now, and five years from now)."* He describes seeing himself with new job responsibilities within a year, seeing himself meeting a partner in two years, and having a child in five years. I tell him to keep this for himself and to now breathe out one time and open his eyes. I instruct him to see the corrected image and what he is to become, once each morning for 21 days, for several seconds (not to exceed a minute) each time.

Clinical Instructions for Correcting a Flashback or Intrusive Memory

Initial Breathing Instructions

Clients sit up as usual with their feet on the floor and their arms on armrests of the chair or in their lap. I use a slightly simpler breathing instruction than for nightmares: "Close your eyes and breathe out three times (i.e., three full respiratory cycles starting with the outbreath), counting backward from three to one, with each outbreath being a new number. At one, see yourself very strong and tall, then breathe out again, and see the one becoming a zero and the zero growing in size and becoming a large mirror."

Instructions During the Exercise

"Looking into the mirror, see the disturbing scene and describe what is happening. What do you see, sense, and feel? How are you correcting the memory, knowing that you have whatever and whomever you need to help you?"

> *Note:* If clients are unable to correct a memory then simply have them wash the troubling scene away, out of the left side of the mirror, using a firefighter's hose. If they are unable to imaginally wash the scene to the left, then have them open their eyes, do several rounds of quieting breath, and instruct them to sense their feet flat on the ground and their backs against the chair, coming back to the present moment calm and relaxed.

Closing Breathing Instructions

"Keeping your eyes closed, breathe out once and, looking into the mirror, see how you have corrected this event with a different past and a new now, seeing how you may become (in one year from now, two years from now, and five years from now). Keep these images for yourself. When you are finished, breathe out and open your eyes."

For Clinicians

> *Note*: Some clients may not be able to see ahead, modify accordingly.

Follow-up

If clients are successful in reversing the memory, fully or partially, or even just comfortable washing the memory out with a hose, and feel confident continuing this on their own, then instruct them as follows:

"Do this imagery exercise each morning, for the next 21 days. Closing your eyes, breathing out three times slowly, see the *corrected* past and what you are to become (a year from now, two years from now, and five years from now). If anything needs to be tweaked or corrected, correct it. Then breathe out and open your eyes. The exercise takes no more than a few seconds to a minute."

> *Final Note*: Treat the above examples and scripts as springboards for you to make your own discoveries in working in this magically transformative realm.

Endnotes

[1] Robert Rhondell Gibson, *Notes on Personal Integration and Health*, 2nd Ed., (Carmel, CA: Rhondell Publishing, 1989), 36.

[2] Gerald Epstein, Healing Visualizations (New York: Bantam Books, 1989), 37.

[3] American Addictions Center Resource, "Anger Symptoms, Causes and Effects," PsychGuides.com, accessed June 22, 2019. https://www.psychguides.com/guides/anger-symptoms-causes-and-effects.

[4] Adapted from Epstein, *Kabbalah for Inner Peace*, 163-164.

[5] Adapted from Benyosef, *Reversing Cancer Through Mental Imagery*, 195–196, 200–201. Also called Nighttime Reserving in Gerald Epstein's, *Healing Visualisations*, 138-139.

[6] Kübler-Ross, *On Death and Dying: What the Dying Have to Teach Doctors, Nurses, Clergy and Their Own Families*, (New York: Simon and Schuster/Touchstone, 1969).

[7] Sae Young Kim, and Yun Young Kim, "Mirror Therapy for Phantom Limb Pain," *The Korean Journal of Pain* 25, no. 4 (2012): 272–274. PMC. doi:10.3344/kjp.2012.25.4.272. See also, researchgate.net/publication/253235147_Mirror_Therapy_Practical_Protocol_for_Stroke_Rehabilitation.

Endnotes

[8] According to the Merriam-Webster dictionary, proprioception is the ability to sense stimuli arising within the body regarding position, motion, and equilibrium. Even if a person is blindfolded, he or she knows through proprioception if an arm is above the head or hanging by the side of the body.

[9] Modern research has shown that the brain and gut are in constant communication. Like the brain, the small intestine is an instinctual thinking organ, alerting us to danger and providing us with gut feelings of intuition. On a physical level, it acts as a gatekeeper, taking in foods that are nourishing and rejecting those that are not. This imagery calls on the gut to heal the brain.

[10] Megan Zottarelli, "Interpreting Data on Military Sexual Assault," *Swords to Plowshares,* May 25, 2015. accessed March 8, 2018, https://www.swords-to-plowshares.org/2015/05/29/interpreting-data-on-military-sexual-assault/.

[11] See Epstein, *Healing Into Immortality,* 222–227, for fuller descriptions of these techniques as well as other techniques of will. Life plan is based on Murile Lasry-Lancri's work.

[12] Adapted from Epstein, *Healing Visualizations,* 208–214.

[13] James S. Gordon, et al., "Treatment of Posttraumatic Stress Disorder in Postwar Kosovar Adolescents Using Mind-body Skills Groups: a Randomized Controlled Trial," *Journal of Clinical Psychiatry,* epub August 2008: 1469-76, accessed June 22, 2019. https://www.ncbi.nlm.nih.gov/pubmed/18945398.

[14] Gerald Epstein, "GEMS Spiritual Healthcare Model," drjerryepstein.org, accessed June 08, 2017. http://drjerryepstein.org/content/gems-spiritual-healthcare-model.

[15] Neuroplasticity or brain plasticity is defined as "the capacity of the nervous system to change its structure and its function over a lifetime, in reaction to environmental diversity. Although this term is now commonly used in psychology and neuroscience, it is not easily defined and is used to refer to changes at many levels in the nervous system ranging from molecular events, such as changes in gene expression, to behavior." CogniFit, "Neuroplasticity: Structure

and Organization," CogniFit.com, accessed March 5, 2018. https://www.cognifit.com/brain-plasticity-and-cognition.

[16] Lev S. Vygotsky, *Thought and Language*, edited by Alex Kozulin (MA: MIT Press, 1986).

[17] Bruce Goldman, "Slow Breathing Induces Tranquility," *Standford Medicine News Center*, March 30, 2017, 1411–1415. https://med.stanford.edu/news/all-news/2017/03/study-discovers-how-slow-breathing-induces-tranquility.html.

[18] Noted neuroscience researcher Nancy Craigmyle, in telephone communication with Dr. Gerald Epstein, 1998.

[19] Deryn Strange and Melanie K. T. Takarangi, "Memory Distortion for Traumatic Events: The Role of Mental Imagery," *Frontiers in Psychiatry* 6 (2015): 27. PMC. https://doi.org/10.3389/fpsyt.2015.00027.

[20] See for example: Ulas Kaplan, Gerald N. Epstein, and Anne Sullivan Smith, "Microdevelopment of Daily Well-Being Through Mental Imagery Practice," *Imagination, Cognition and Personality* 34, no. 1 (October 10, 2014): 73–96. https://doi.org/10.2190/IC.34.1.f; Ulas Kaplan and Gerald Epstein, "Psychophysiological Coherence as a Function of Mental Imagery Practice, *Imagination, Cognition and Personality* 31, no. 4 (November 1, 2012): 297–312. http://doi:10.2190/ic.31.4.d; Gerald Epstein et al., "A Pilot Study of Mind-Body Changes in Adults with Asthma who Practice Mental Imagery," *Alternative Therapies in Health and Medicine*, 10 (July/August 2004): 66-71. https://www.researchgate.net/publication/8425251_A_pilot_study_of_mind-body_changes_in_adults_with_asthma_who_practice_mental_imagery; and Gerald Epstein et al., "Alleviating Asthma With Mental Imagery: A Phenomenological Approach," *Alternative and Complementary Therapies* 3, No. 1 (January 1997): 42–52. https://doi.org/10.1089/act.1997.3.42.

[21] Gerald Epstein, "Your Dreams," drjerryepstein.org, accessed March 07, 2018. http://drjerryepstein.org/your-dreams. See also, Gerald Epstein, *Waking Dream Therapy: Dream Process as Imagination* (New York: Human Sciences Press, 1981, Reprinted New York: ACMI Press 1992).

Sources of Imagery

In addition to the imagery exercises we composed, we were fortunate to have access to many imagery exercises authored by Mme. Colette Aboulker-Muscat and Dr. Gerald Epstein. These exercises were drawn and adapted from their published works, private notes, and personal communications. We are deeply grateful to them for sharing their wisdom and knowledge so freely with us throughout the years.

Additionally, we are thankful to Simcha Benyosef (Staircases of Life, Freed Prisoner, Orange Tree, Reversing the Conflicts of the Day, Shampooing the Brain), Judy Besserman (Forest of Forgiveness, Jail of Guilt), Sarah Berkovits (Stone of Fear), Dr. Elizabeth Barrett (The Flashlight), and Sara Esterabadeyan (Rainbow Staircase) for allowing us to adapt and share several of their imagery exercises. Thanks also to Paul Simon (Diamonds on the Soles of Your Feet, Bouncing into Graceland) and to Rumi/Coleman Barks (The Guest House) for inspiring several imagery exercises.

References

Aboulker-Muscat, Colette. *Ten Exercises*. Directed by Patrick Bokanowski. Performed by Colette Aboulker-Muscat. France: Re:Voir, 2008. DVD.

Aboulker-Muscat, Colette. *The Waking Dream*. Directed by Patrick Bokanowski. Performed by Colette Aboulker-Muscat. France: Re:Voir, 2008. DVD.

Benyosef, Simcha H. *Reversing Cancer Through Mental Imagery*. New York: ACMI Press, 2017.

Berkovits, Sarah. *Guided Imagery with Children: Successful Techniques to Improve School Performance and Self-Esteem*. Duluth, MN: Whole Persons Associates, 2005.

Epstein, Gerald. "Mental Imagery Exercises." www.drjerryepstein.com. Accessed June 20, 2019. https://www.drjerryepstein.org/exercises.

References

Epstein, Gerald N., Elizabeth Ann Manhart Barrett, James P. Halper, Nathan S. Seriff, Kim Phillips, and Stephen Lowenstein. "Alleviating Asthma with Mental Imagery." *Alternative and Complementary Therapies* 3, no. 1 (January 01, 1997): 42–52. http://doi:10.1089/act.1997.3.42 .

Epstein, Gerald N., James P. Halper, Elizabeth Ann Manhart Barrett, Carole Birdsall, Monnie McGee, Kim P. Baron, and Stephen Lowenstein. "A Pilot Study of Mind–Body Changes in Adults with Asthma Who Practice Mental Imagery." *Alternative Therapies in Health and Medicine* 10, no. 4 (July 2004): 66–71. https://www.researchgate.net/publication/8425251_A_pilot_study_of_mind-body_changes_in_adults_with_asthma_who_practice_mental_imagery.

Epstein, Gerald, and Barbarah L. Fedoroff, eds. *Encyclopedia of Mental Imagery: Colette Aboulker-Muscat — 2,100 Visualizations for Personal Development, Healing and Self-Knowledge.* New York: ACMI Press, 2012.

Epstein, Gerald. *Healing Into Immortality: A New Spiritual Medicine of Healing Stories and Imagery.* New York: ACMI Press, 2010.

Epstein, Gerald. *Healing Visualizations: Creating Health Through Imagery.* New York: Bantam Books, 1989.

Epstein, Gerald. "How to Use Mental Imagery for Any Clinical Condition: Some Relevant Pointers." In *Healing Images: The Role of Imagination in Health*, edited by Anees Sheikh, 427-436. New York: Baywood Publishers, 2003.

Epstein, Gerald. *Kabbalah for Inner Peace: Imagery and Insights to Guide You Through Your Day*. New York: ACMI Press, 2008.

Epstein, Gerald. *The Natural Laws of Self-Healing: Harnessing Your Inner Imaging Power to Reach Spirit*. Wheeling, Illinois: Nightingale Conant, 2003. Audio CD set.

Epstein, Gerald. *The Phoenix Process: One Minute a Day to Health, Longevity, and Well-Being*. Wheeling, Illinois: Nightingale Conant, 2007. Audio CD set.

Epstein, Gerald. *Waking Dream Therapy: Dream Process as Imagination*. New York: Human Sciences Press, 1981. Reprint *Waking Dream Therapy: Unlocking the Secrets of Self through Dreams and Imagination*. New York: ACMI Press, 2000.

Epstein, Gerald. "The Western Metaphysics of Mental Imagery and its Clinical Application." In *Transformative Imagery: Cultivating the Imagination for Healing, Change, and Growth*, edited by Leslie Davenport, 59–72. London: Jessica Kingsley, 2016.

References

Gibson, Robert Rhondell. *Notes on Personal Integration and Health*. Second ed. Carmel, CA: Rhondell Publishing, 1989. Available at http://www.rhondell.com/catalog.htm.

Goldman, Bruce. "Study Shows How Slow Breathing Induces Tranquility." Stanford Medicine News Center. March 30, 2017. https://med.stanford.edu/news/all-news/2017/03/study-discovers-how-slow-breathing-induces-tranquility.html.

Gordon, James S., Julie K. Staples, Afrim Blyta, Murat Bytyqi, and Amy T. Wilson. "Treatment of Posttraumatic Stress Disorder in Postwar Kosovar Adolescents Using Mind-body Skills Groups: a Randomized Controlled Trial." *Journal of Clinical Psychiatry*, epub August 2008:1469-76. https://www.ncbi.nlm.nih.gov/pubmed/18945398.

Kaplan, Ulas, Gerald N. Epstein, and Anne Sullivan Smith. "Microdevelopment of Daily Well-Being Through Mental Imagery Practice." *Imagination, Cognition and Personality* 34, no. 1 (October 10, 2014): 73–96. https://doi.org/10.2190/IC.34.1.f.

Kaplan, Ulas, and Gerald N. Epstein. "Psychophysiological Coherence as a Function of Mental Imagery Practice." *Imagination, Cognition and Personality* 31, no. 4 (November 1, 2012): 297–312. https://doi.org/10.2190/IC.31.4.d.

Kim, Sae Young, and Yun Young Kim. "Mirror Therapy for Phantom Limb Pain." *The Korean Journal of Pain* 25.4 (2012): 272–274. PMC. doi:10.3344/kjp.2012.25.4.272.

Kübler-Ross, Elisabeth. *On Death and Dying: What the Dying Have to Teach Doctors, Nurses, Clergy and Their Own Families.* New York: Simon and Schuster/Touchstone, 1969.

Rūmī, Jalāl Al-Dīn. *The Essential Rumi.* Translated by Coleman Barks and John Moyne. San Francisco, CA: HarperSanFrancisco, 1995.

Simon, Paul. "Diamonds on the Soles of Her Shoes." *Graceland.* New York: Warner Bros, 1986. Audio CD.

Simon, Paul. "Graceland." *Graceland.* New York: Warner Bros., 1986. Audio CD.

Strange, Deryn, and Melanie K. T. Takarangi. "Memory Distortion for Traumatic Events: The Role of Mental Imagery." *Frontiers in Psychiatry* 6 (2015): 27. *PMC.* doi: 10.3389/fpsyt.2015.00027.

Vygotsky, Lev S. *Thought and Language*, edited by Alex Kozulin. Rev. Ed. Cambridge, MA: MIT Press, 1986.

Zottarelli, Megan. "Interpreting Data on Military Sexual Assault." Swords to Plowshares. May 29, 2015. Accessed March 8, 2018. https://www.swords-to-plowshares.org/2015/05/29/interpreting-data-on-military-sexual-assault/.

Main Index

Aboulker-Muscat, Colette, xi, xiv, 195
acupuncture, 112
addiction, 135-136, 154-158
    imagery exercises for, 75, 137-141, 154-158
    See also alcohol use; drug use
Afghanistan war. *See* Operation Enduring Freedom
alcohol use, 70, 98, 135-137, 143, 144, 156
    clinical cases involving, 10, 71, 136
    mood disorders and, 70
    See also Life Plan; reversing; stopping exercises
anger, 45-48
    clinical examples of, 7, 27, 47, 70, 159, 182
    exercises for, imagery, 49-54
        physical, 55
anti-depressants. *See* depression; prescription drugs
anxiety, general, xxiii, 2, 35-36, 45
    clinical examples of, xviii, 12, 14, 37, 48, 57, 66, 71, 181-182, 187-189
        crowds, among, 12-13, 14, 27, 145, 160
        driving, 27, 187-189
    imagery exercises for, 33, 38-44, 74, 88, 120, 133, 149 (*see also* reversing)
    See also hypervigilance, triggers
appetite, loss of, 70, 128, 145. *See also* eating disorders
art therapy, xx

blue nucleus. *See* locus coeruleus
brain science. *See* neurology
breath work, 14-15, 178. *See also* neurology; pacemaker for breathing
breathing techniques, 17-19

cerebral hemisphere, right and left, 2
clinical depression, 71. *See also* depression
concentration problems, 70, 127, 143
    clinical examples of, 27, 71, 136
concussion. *See* mild Traumatic Brain Injury
correction, making a, 28-29, 167, 181
    clinical examples of, 29, 181-182, 182-184, 187-189
    See also reversing
cutting. *See* self-harm

depressants, 70, 135. *See also* alcohol use
depression, xiii, 2, 69-72, 160, 169
    alcohol use and, 135
    clinical, 71
    exercises for, imagery, 72-76
        physical, 77-78
    five stages of grief and, 108
    mild Traumatic Brain Injury and, 127
    pain and, 112
    patient examples of, 70-71, 80
    physical exercises for, 77-78
    symptoms of, 70, 71
    See also Veterans Crisis Hotline
despair, xiii, xiv, 70
    imagery exercises for, 73-75, 168
    See also depression
direct seeing, 11
disorder. *See* eating disorders; mood disorder; Post-Traumatic Stress Disorder;
        sleep-related disorder
distress, xxiii, 4
    as symptom of depression, 70
    clinical examples of, 8, 38, 106

Index

       imagery exercises for, 20, 154, 163-164
       odors which cause, 61
       reversing, 46-47, 154-155
       sleep disorders and, 97
drug use, 70, 98, 135-137, 143, 144
       clinical examples of, 136
       imagery exercises for overcoming, 137-141
       mood disorders and, 70
       See also Life Plan; prescription drugs; stopping exercises

eating disorders, 144, 158. *See also* appetite, loss of
Epstein, Gerald, ix, xiii-xv, xix, 195
exercises. *See* mirror exercises; physical exercises; *Index of Mental Imagery Exercises*
Eye Movement Desensitization and Reprocessing (EMDR), xx

false emergency state, 3
       exercise to address response to, 59
       See also PTSD
families of veterans, exercises for, 160-167
Feldenkrais, 112
flashbacks, 187
       clinical examples, 187-189
       imagery exercises for, 189-191

Gibson, Robert Rhondell, 3. *See also* false emergency state
grief, 105-108
       clinical examples of, 106, 107
       exercises for, imagery, 108-110
              physical, 110-111
       five stages of, 108
       religious mourning and, 105-106
guided imagery. *See* mental imagery
guilt, 79-82
       clinical examples of, 27, 71, 79-82, 106
       imagery exercises for, 83-85, 109-110
       versus remorse versus regret, 81

See also mirror exercises; reversing
Gulf War, 56
    veterans' stories, 38, 100-101, 127-128, 144-145

hypervigilance, 4, 26-29, 56, 91, 143
    clinical examples of, 7, 66, 93-94
    imagery exercises for, 30-34
    See also triggers
hypnotherapy, xviii, xx, 177, 178

imaginal thinking, 1-5
insomnia, 91
    clinical examples of, 7-13-14, 26-27, 38, 66, 71, 92, 93-94, 100, 113, 128, 145, 187-189
    exercises for, imagery 93-97
        physical, 104
    See also nightmares; reversing
Iraq War, 177
    veterans' stories, 12, 26, 66, 70, 79, 160, 187

Korean War, 56
    veteran's story, 6
Kubler-Ross, Elisabeth, 108

Life Plan, 5, 137, 154-157
locus coeruleus, 178
logical thinking vs imaginal thinking, 1-2
loss. *See* grief

mantras, xx
massage, 112
    used in imagery exercise, 40
meditation, xix, xx, 3, 21, 177, 178
mental imagery
    Aboulker-Muscat, Colette and, xiv-xv
    basic steps of practice, 17-22
    breathing and, 17-19

Index

    cardinal rules of, 16
    definition of, 1
    direct seeing and, 11
    Epstein, Gerald, and, xi, xiii-xv, xix, 168-170, 181
    Life Plan and, 154-157
    meditation and, 21, 177-178
    neurology and, 3, 177-179
    philosophy of, 8-12
    religion and, 2
    stopping exercises in, 157-158
    tips for practicing, 23-25
    See also Aboulker-Muscat, Colette; Epstein, Gerald; imaginal thinking; retracing the past; *Index of Mental Imagery Exercises*

mild Traumatic Brain Injury, 127- 128, 177
    clinical examples of, 92, 127-128
    imagery exercises for, 128-134

mindbody medicine, 176-177

mirror exercises
    imaginal, 87-90
    phantom limb pain, 123-125

mood disorders, 70. *See also* depression

neurasthenia, xiv. *See also* PTSD

neurology
    cerebral hemisphere, right and left, 2
    locus coeruleus, 178
    minor Traumatic Brain Injury (mTBI) and, 127-128, 177
    mirror exercises and, 123-124
    neuroplasticity, 3, 177-178
    norepinephrine, 18-19
    pacemaker for breathing, 178
    parasympathetic nervous system, 4
    peripheral noradrenaline, 178

neuroplasticity, 3, 177-178

nightmares, 91, 100-101
    clinical examples of, xviii, 7, 27, 48, 100, 145, 181-182, 182-184

imagery exercises for, 101-104, 184-186
	See also correcting; insomnia
night terrors, 91
norepinephrine, 18-19

occupational therapy, clinical use of, 128
Operation Enduring Freedom, 177
	veterans' stories, 14, 47-48, 92, 105-107, 113
Operation Iraqi Freedom. *See* Iraq War

pacemaker for breathing, 178
pain, physical, 112-113
	addiction and, 135
	clinical examples of, 92, 113, 128, 136
	imagery exercises for, 114-123
	sleep and, 91-92
	See also phantom pain
parasympathetic nervous system, 4
Parker, Diane, 147-148
peripheral noradrenaline, 178
phantom pain, 123-124
	imagery exercises for, 124-126
physical therapy, 112, 128
Post-Traumatic Stress Disorder (PTSD)
	alcohol and, 70, 98, 135-137, 143, 144, 156
	characteristics of, xix, 2
	family members and, 159-160
	history of, xiv, xviii
	neurology and, 3-5, 177-179
	patterns of recurrence, 7
	treatment alternatives to mental imagery, xiv, xviii-xx, 176-177
	See also false emergency state, neurasthenia, shell shock, war
		neurosis, war trauma
prescription drugs, xiv, xviii, 92

religion, mental imagery and, 2
	mourning and, 105-106

Index

       patient experience with, 12
reparations, 82. *See also* guilt
repentance, definition, 85. *See also* guilt; "Repentance" in *Index of Mental Imagery Exercises*
retracing the past, xiv. *See also* Aboulker-Muscat, Colette; mental imagery
reversing, techniques for, 97-100, 182-191
       See also mirror exercises; stopping exercises
rewiring the brain. *See* neuroplasticity
right cerebral hemisphere, 2

San Diego Vet Center, xi, xv, xx, xxi, 180
       patient experiences at, 6, 26, 47, 56, 171
San Diego Veterans Court, 47
Schrödinger, Erwin, 177
shell shock, xiv. *See also* PTSD
self-harm, 69, 144. *See also* suicide
self-medication. *See* addiction; alcohol use; drug use
sexual trauma, 142-146
       imagery exercises for, 146-153
       symptoms of victims of, 143-144
sleep-related disorder, 91
sleeping trouble. *See* insomnia
somatic experience training, xx, 124, 177, 178
Stanford University School of Medicine, 178
stopping exercises, 157-158
stress hormones. *See* norepinephrine; peripheral noradrenaline
suicide, 69
       patients' thoughts of, 71, 80, 145
       Veterans Crisis Hotline, 69

tai chi, xx
talk therapy, xiv, xx, 176
therapy. *See* art therapy; hypnotherapy; occupational therapy; physical therapy; talk therapy
tinnitus, 92, 132, 133
tranquilizers. *See* prescription drugs
Traumatic Brain Injury. *See* mild Traumatic Brain Injury

triggers, 56-58
    clinical examples of, xviii, 6, 57, 160
    imagery exercises for, 58-64
        driving, 61-62
        noise, 62-64
        safety, 58-59
        smells, 60-61

vestibular therapy, 128
Veterans Crisis Hotline, 69
Vietnam War, xiv, 56
    veterans' stories, 36-37, 56-57, 107-108, 135-136, 159-160, 182-183
    exercise for veterans of, 64
visualization. *See* mental imagery
Vygotsky, Lev, 177

Walter Reed National Military Medical Center, 79
war. *See* Gulf War; Iraq War; Korean War; Operation Enduring Freedom;
        Vietnam War
war neurosis, xiv. *See also* PTSD
war trauma, xiv, 3, 16, 27, 66, 176, 181. *See also* PTSD
yoga, xix, xx

zones of proximal development, 177

Index of PTSD Patient Stories
Organized by Difficulty Experienced*

alcohol or drug use, 10, 71, 136
anger, 7, 10, 27, 47, 70, 159, 182-184
anxiety, general, xviii, 12, 14, 37, 57, 71, 181-182, 187-189
concentration difficulty, 136
crowds, fear of, 12-13, 14, 27, 145, 160
depression, 70-71, 80
eating struggles, 128, 145
fear, general, 37, 48
       triggered by: driving, 27, 187-189; smells, 57; sound, xviii, 6, 57, 160
grief, 106, 107
guilt, 80, 106
hypervigilance, xviii, 7, 26-28, 66, 93-94
isolation, 66
nightmares, xviii, 7, 27, 48, 100, 145, 181-182, 182-184
pain, physical, 92, 113, 128, 136
sleeping trouble, 7, 13-14, 26-28, 38, 66, 71, 92, 93-94, 100, 113, 128, 145, 187-189
suicidal thoughts, 80, 145

*All of the patient stories described in this book, with the exception of Dr. Kahaney's, use a fictional name.

Index of Mental Imagery Exercises

Aladdin's Turban, 129
The Anger Speedometer, 50
Atlas Shrugged, 161

Bells and Chimes, 133
The Black Hole, 73
Blowing Away the Dark Clouds, 72
Blue Blood, 49
Blue Sky Umbrella, 74, 161
Bouncing into Graceland, 109-110
      source: Paul Simon, 195
Breathing As One, 162-163

Challenger Deep, 147-148
The Chariot, 61-62
Cheering from the Stands, 62-63
Chinese Clay Warriors, 96-97
Clean a Space, 78
Cleansing Shower, 23-24
Cleansing the Heart, 172-173
Clear Water, 40
      clinical use, 37-38
Clearing the Tears, 109
Cloak, 146
Clothing Choice, 77

Index

The Cocoon, 67-68
Coming Out of the Shadows, 67
Conquering the Dragon of Fear, 102-103
correcting exercises
    for flashbacks or intrusive memory, 189-191
        clinical example, 187-189
    for nightmares, 184-187
        clinical example, 181-182, 182-183
Creating Your Own Natural "Pain-killer" Exercise, 122-123
The Crystal Light, 116

De-armoring, 33-34
Deep Cleansing from Childhood, 76
Diamonds on the Soles of Your Feet, 153
    source: Paul Simon, 195
Drawing Spirals, 78
The Drop of Hope, 74-75

Emerald Dome, 43, 95-96

Falling Out of Adversity, 119
The Fireman's Hose, 50-51
The Flashlight, 130-131
    source: Dr. Elizabeth Barrett, 195
The Forest of Forgiveness, 53-54
    source: Judy Besserman, 195
Freed Prisoner, 52
    source: Simcha Benyosef, 195

The Garden of Eden, 150-151, 161
Golden Ladder, 137-138
Golden Lasso, 149
Golden Net, 42
The Green Ball, 51
Green Leaf, 117-118
Green Meadow, 118-119

The Guest House, 68
       source: Rumi/Coleman Books, 195

Heartache, 120, 139
Heavy Hands, 116
Helicopter Trigger Exercise, 64
Hurling into Space, 114

Inner Journey, 140-141
       clinical use, 136
The Inside Observer, 149-150

The Jail of Guilt, 84
       source: Judy Besserman, 195

The Lake of Tears, 147
The Lake of the Brain, 132

Laying the Dead to Rest, 108-109
Life and Light, 173-174
Life Can Be a Bed of Roses, 60
Life Plan, 154-157

The Magnet of Health, 121
The Matrix of Healing, 129
Melody of Life, 63
The Milky Way of Health, 123
Mirror Exercise, 77
mirror exercises
       for phantom limb pain, 123-125
       imaginal, 87-90
       See also Replacing the Bad with the Good; The War Within
The Movie Channel, 103-104
The Mummy, 175
My Sweet Heaven, 59

Index

Net Worth Exercise, 165
Noose of Anger, 49-50

The Octopus, 117
Orange Tree, 128-129
    source: Simcha Benyosef, 195
The Orchid, 151-152

Painless Voyage, 115
Pendulum, 38-39
    clinical use, 38
The Perimeter Check, 94
    clinical use, 187
physical exercises
    for anger, 55
    for bereavement, 110-111
    for depression, 77-78
    for hypervigilance, 34
    for protection, 104
    for smell triggers, 61
    See also Unfolding the Day, 166-167
Protection, 95

The Question Mark, 114

Ra, 75, 139
    clinical use, 136
Rainbow Staircase, 148
    source: Sara Esterabadeyan, 195
Red Ribbon, 83
The Red Sea Parting/Safe Passage, 30, 62
    clinical use, 187-189
Reimagining Yourself, 173
Remembering Love, 53
Repentance: Reversing Errors of the Past, 86-87
Replacing the Bad with the Good, 88
    See also mirror exercises: imaginal

Reversing Anger, 51-52
Reversing the Day, 97-100
    source: Simcha Benyosef, 195
reversing imagery exercises
    clinical use, 87, 180-182
        See also correcting exercises; mirror exercises; stopping exercises
Ring of Fire, 32, 96
Room of Silence, 41, 63, 13

Sand Salutation, 42, 160
Sandpaper, 122,
The Seashore, 22
    tips for practicing, 24-25
Seeing Yourself Whole, 124-126
Self-Renewal, 34
    See also The Garden of Eden
Serpent in the Sun, 138-139
The Setting Sun, 93
    clinical use, 92
Shampooing the Brain 131
    source: Simcha Benyosef, 195
Sitting Through Anger, 54-55
Staircases of Life, 43-44
    source: Simcha Benyosef, 195
Steel Wall, 32
Sticks of Light, 146
Stone of Fear, 40
    clinical use 37-8
    source: Sarah Berkovits, 195
stopping exercises 154, 157-158
Stress Without Distress, 163-165
Strong Box, 102
The Superhero, 33
Swallowing the Rainbow, 73

Take Me to the River, 85
The Tidal Wave, 31

Index

The Tree of Life, 60
Through the Jungle, 134
Through the Magnifying Glass, 115

Unfolding the Day: Directing Your Will to Benefit Yourself, 166-167
Un-Triggering Yourself, 58

Valley of Peace, 133
Vase of Blue Light, 130

Walking Straight, Walking Tall, 139
The War Within, 90
    See also mirror exercises: imaginal
The White Silk Cape, 161

Reversing the Trauma of War

About the Authors

Phyllis Kahaney, MSW, PhD

After successfully overcoming the symptoms of PTSD using mental imagery, she shifted the direction of her professional life in academia as a Professor of English to work in the healing arts using mental imagery. She obtained a master of social work at San Diego State University and studied privately with Dr. Gerald Epstein and Mme. Colette Aboulker-Muscat. Her studies culminated in her work as a readjustment counselor at the San Diego Vet Center, where she worked with combat veterans with diagnoses of PTSD and traumatic brain injury. Currently she works in hospice providing end-of-life care in San Diego.

Rachel Epstein, LAc, JD

Rachel is the director of the American Institute for Mental Imagery and a holistic health practitioner with a private practice in New York City. She conducts classes on mental imagery, which she learned from internationally recognized authorities Mme. Colette Aboulker-Muscat and Dr. Gerald Epstein, M.D., her late husband with whom she collaborated on numerous books and trainings. She is a licensed acupuncturist trained in Traditional Chinese Medicine and has a juris doctorate from Benjamin N. Cardozo School of Law.